If You're a Tomato I'll Ketchup With You

Tomato Gardening Tips and Tricks

Easy-Growing Gardening Guide, Vol. 3

Rosefiend Cordell

Rosefiend Publishing

ISBN: 978-1-953196-13-2

ALL THE BOOKS I'VE WRITTEN SO FAR

The Easy-Growing Gardening Series
Don't Throw in the Trowel: Vegetable Gardening Month by Month
Rose to the Occasion: An Easy-Growing Guide to Rose Gardening
If You're a Tomato, I'll Ketchup With You: Tomato Gardening Tips and Tricks
Perennial Classics: Planting and Growing Great Perennial Gardens
Petal to the Metal: Growing Gorgeous Houseplants
Gardening Month by Month: Tips for Great Flowers, Vegetables, & Houseplants
Leave Me A Lawn: Lawn Care for Tired Gardeners
Japanese Beetles and Grubs: Trap, Spray, Control Them
Stay Grounded: Soil Building for Sustainable Gardens
Genius Gardening Hacks: Tips and Fixes for the Creative Gardener
Design of the Times: How to Plan Glorious Landscapes and Gardens

Civil War Books
Courageous Women of the Civil War: Soldiers, Spies, Medics, and More (Chicago Review Press, 2016)
Gentlemen, Accept This Facial Hair Challenge! Epic Beards and Moustaches of the Civil War

The Dragonriders of Skala series (written with Pauline Creeden)
The Flame of Battle
A Fire of Roses
A Crown of Flames
A Whisper of Smoke (a stand-alone prequel)

Young Adult Novels
Angel in the Whirlwind
Butterfly Chaos
Those Black Wings
Why Can't My Life Be a Romance Novel? A goofy romantic short
Fifteen Inches Tall and Bulletproof: Ten Short Stories

The White Oak Chronicles:
The Chieftain (a stand-alone prequel)
Outlander's Scar
Wandering Stars
Silverlady Descends

DEDICATION

To Dad, who always used to sing a bit of a jingle from an old commercial: "If you're a tomato I'll ketchup with you." I've never found out what commercial that was from, but it's a good line. It gets stuck in my head from time to time. I'm fine with that.

CONTENTS

IF YOU'RE A TOMATO I'LL KETCHUP WITH YOU

Gardening is cheaper than therapy -- and you get tomatoes.

TOMATO VARIETIES

The National Gardening Association has found that, among vegetable gardeners, tomatoes are their favorite plant to grow. One in three Americans have a vegetable garden, and 9 out of 10 of those gardens have tomatoes in them.

In January and February, when spring fever is really hitting hard, those heirloom seed catalogs inspire dreams of the perfect vegetable garden and the veritable cornucopia of delicious vegetables that it will pour upon our collective tables. Not literally of course, as that would be a mess. But man, those seed catalog tomatoes. It wouldn't be so bad if the seed catalogs could offer taste samples of everything.

When I flip through the Baker Creek seed catalog, which is far and away my favorite, they offer 13 pages of tomatoes (and one page of tomatillos). And so many heirloom varieties. Who knew there was such a variety of tomatoes? Green tomatoes, orange tomatoes, pink tomatoes. Here are the purple, black, and brown tomatoes, which include Black Krim, Cherokee Purple, Paul Robeson, and True Black Brandywine. They have red tomatoes, naturally, two pages of striped tomatoes, two pages of Brad Gate's multicolored tomatoes, some of which are downright psychedelic in purples, yellows, reds, and browns. Then we have blue tomatoes (actually rich purples) and white tomatoes (a very pale yellow, like Bunnicula had been at work on them), and of course yellow tomatoes. I had a Yellow Pear tomato plant that took over half my garden. I can appreciate that kind of vigor in my plants. You can also get peach tomatoes, which have a light layer of fuzz.

Tomatoes also range in size from gigantic beefsteak tomatoes that can weigh up to a half-pound, to the smallest cherry tomato about the size of a marble. You can grow heavy-yielding hybrids or open-pollinated heirloom varieties in different colors, shades, and sizes. You can choose early varieties that set fruit when it's cool outside, mid-season varieties, and late-maturing varieties that will give you the biggest fruits but take 80 to 90 days to do it. Sometimes you'll need about 120 days to get a decent harvest, but hey, at least you get tomatoes!

Tomatoes are so versatile and so good. You can cook them a million different ways or you can eat them, sun-warmed and delicious, straight off the vine. Some people grab a cherry tomato, a leaf of basil, and a slice of mozzarella cheese, and eat them like that.

Determinate vs. Indeterminate

I've known about these two different kinds of tomatoes for decades and yet I still can't keep them straight in my head. It's like the difference between flammable and inflammable, kind of.

Determinate tomatoes produce fruit at the ends of their branches. These will stop growing when they are still pretty short.

Indeterminate tomatoes bear fruit along their stems, which keep growing and growing and growing.

If you want a little short tomato to grow in a pot on your patio, get a determinate one.

If you want a Godzilla tomato to take over the world, get an indeterminate one.

STARTING TOMATOES FROM SEED

If you start tomatoes from seed, it's best to start them inside, whether on a window sill or in a cold frame. At any rate, tomatoes need a soil temperature of at least 60 degrees to germinate, though they prefer warmer temperatures, up to 80 degrees. It's a sure bet that your outdoor soil temperature aren't going to get that high any time soon!

Tomato seeds need to be started six to eight weeks before the last frost date.

You can start Early Girl tomatoes (or any early tomato variety) under lights as early as February, then, when the weather is mild enough, transplant to the garden with a Wall o' Waters to help protect the plants against all the frosts.

Traditionally, in Missouri, zone 5, this date has been May 15. With global warming as it is, that date can be moved back to May 1, and even earlier. (Old gardening wisdom is always helpful, but still needs to be updated from time to time.)

So get out your calendar and count back six or eight weeks from your frost date, and that's your sowing date.

(Protip: Keep a gardening calendar and notebook where you write down things like sowing dates, the dates you see frost, etc., and use them next winter when you're planning for the next planting year.)

Next, line up your planting containers. Whether you use old egg cartons, Solo cups, flower pots, have them scrubbed (well, don't scrub the egg cartons) if you're reusing them. (Cleaning up the trays/flower pots will clean up any diseases that might be harbored there – diseases that could affect your young seedlings. Use hot water, soap, and a dash of bleach.)

Be sure that, whatever you use, your planter has plenty of drainage holes! This is not negotiable!

For seeds, it's best to use a light seeding mix that is high in vermiculite, though not necessary. A regular "soilless" potting mix is fine. The seeding mix, which is more expensive, also is lighter and easier for newly-germinated seedlings to poke their little green heads through.

When I ran a greenhouse, I started my seedlings in trays and then transplanted them to six packs and four packs later on when they were big enough. For small windowsill operations, this won't be necessary. You can put some soil in a small Solo cup (with drainage holes poked into the bottom), stick two or three tomato seeds in there, and let 'em grow until they're big enough to transplant directly into the garden.

The tomato seeds will germinate more effectively if you have a heat mat under the cups or trays. This will warm the soil with dependable heat, allowing the seedlings to germinate more quickly and grow out more quickly. Just be sure to get a thermostat with the mats so you can adjust the temperature so you don't end up cooking your seeds.

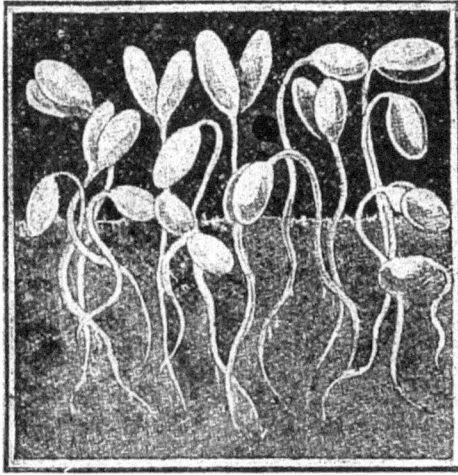

How to Plant Tomato Seeds

Fill your pots, cups, etc. with potting mix, leaving about a half-inch to an inch at the top. Poke two seeds into the middle, about a quarter-inch deep, and cover them. Two seeds are just insurance, just in case one doesn't sprout. When they get bigger, pinch out the wimpier seedling and let the larger one grow.

Gently pack the soil in around the seeds, as seed-to-soil contact is very important for good germination rates.

Sprinkle water on the soil, and keep the soil moist. Don't let it dry out, and don't let it get soggy all the time. Having the soil dry out will kill the seedlings, and constantly wet soil will rot them.

Now one way to keep the soil from drying out is to cover the trays or pots with plastic wrap. This is an easy way to keep the soil moist. Just don't leave the trays in direct sunlight. One time I had the soil covered this way on one of my flats. I came in from one of my jobs and realized that it had been sitting in the sun all afternoon. I ran over and lifted up the plastic wrap – and steam puffed out. Those seeds were roasted!

Once the seeds germinate, though, be sure to remove the plastic wrap, and also have a small fan to keep the air circulating a little around them. Seedling are susceptible to a disease called "damping off" which is encouraged by poor air circulation.

Damping-Off Disease

I had a bout of damping-off disease in my greenhouse, and it was a mess. Damping-off is a fungal disease that causes newly-planted seedlings to keel over and melt away. It spreads out in a circle, as most funguses do (consider "fairy rings," which are circles of mushrooms on the forest floor), killing off seedlings as it spreads outward.

I haven't had damping-off before, since I keep stuff more on the dry side in the greenhouse, which the fungus doesn't like. However, we had cloudy, cold weather for a whole week, and my trays of seedlings, watered on a Sunday, would not dry out for the rest of the week. No sun, and I couldn't turn on the fans to pull the air through because it was too cold. Humidity was high. All the conditions were right for the fungus to strike.

Then the disease got into the snapdragons I'd just planted and started knocking them out everywhere. I called everyone I could think of for help. Then I took their advice, and it worked.

The best defense is a good offense. Keep a fan running at all times to keep the air circulating. You should feel the air moving through the whole room, but you don't have to turn it up so high that it blows the mice out from under the floor. Keep the plants spaced apart to let air move between them. The fungus likes high humidity and temperatures about 70 degrees. The fan keeps the humidity and temperature lower.

This will break your heart, but get rid of everything that's infected by the fungus. Dump out the soil and plants, and take the waste outside so spores won't reinfect the plants. As soon as you see the plant keel over, and you know it's not due to being underwatered, out it goes.

Hardening Off the Seedlings

Once the seedlings get big and husky, and once the weather warms up outside, it's time to harden off the seedlings so they can get acclimated to the weather outside. Plants do better if they have a little time to adjust to the cold temperatures, and the sun, and the wind.

About a week or two before you plan on planting them outside, start moving them outside for a little while. On the first couple of days, water them, then set them outside in the shade in a protected, warm area for an hour or two, then bring them back inside. Then slowly increase exposure to the sun and wind, leaving them out three hours, or four. Then, when you are close to planting time, leave them outside overnight several times (but only if the temperature is supposed to stay over 50 degrees all night). You can harden them off to 40 or 45 degrees if it's sunny out.

While you're hardening them off, keep an eye on them to make sure they're not wilting or drying out.

When they're inside, reduce the amount of water you give them, and don't fertilize them until you plant them in the garden.

Don't worry if you miss a day, and don't stress about "not doing it right." Plants are often tougher than we give them credit for, and often there's no real "right way" or "wrong way." Sometimes regular life gets in the way, so if you can't put your seedlings out every single day, it's okay, just put them out when you can.

PLANTING TOMATOES!

FINALLY FINALLY FINALLY FINALLY FINALLY

Okay, I totally understand the excitement. When's the best time to plant your tomatoes, though?

Tomatoes are warm weather plants. A lot of folks will try to plant them early, and who can blame them. Unfortunately, if the soil temperature is still below 50 degrees, the tomato is not going to grow. The tomato plant is like a cold-blooded person who drapes herself over a heater in winter, and in summer is outside enjoying the heat of the sun.

Tomato plants do best when nighttime temperatures consistently stay above 50 degrees, and when the soil temperature stays above 60 degrees. I don't expect you to carry a soil thermometer around (though I believe one gets gardening points for having one), so here's a rule of thumb (or finger): if you can stick your finger in the soil and leave it there for a full minute without feeling uncomfortable from the cold, then it's ready to plant.

And if the soil temperature is not quite 60 degrees, well, you can still do a few things for that.

PLANTING EARLY BECAUSE YOU JUST CAN'T WAIT

So okay, we'll extend the season.

Warm up the soil. If you've had mulch over your garden all winter (which is a really good idea, because worms go crazy for that stuff and leave worm castings everywhere, which is super-good for your plants), then clear the mulch away and let the sun warm the soil. To help the sun along, lay black plastic on the soil. This will raise the soil temperature by several degrees. You can even leave the plastic on the soil when you're planting your tomatoes. You can leave it there all season, but a layer of organic mulch (grass clippings, chopped-up leaves) is much better for your plants.

Plant in raised beds. If you have raised beds, stick your early tomatoes in there and get them going.

Showing field set with
Hotkaps

Wall of Water/Frost Jackets/Hotkaps – These are plastic dealies (that's scientific terminology for "thingies") that you put up around your tomato plant and fill with water. They absorb light from the sun all day, then release that heat to your plant at night. The top of the Wall o' Waters/Frost Jackets/HotKaps will lean together and cover up your plant like a blue (or red) water teepee. These seem to be available widely and work nicely. Set them up a week before you plan to plant your tomatoes to warm the soil where you plant to put your plants. You can leave them on your tomatoes until 30 to 45 days after your last frost date, and it won't overheat your tomato plant. (In May, tomatoes aren't going to overheat anyway, but they luxuriate in the warmth.)

Milk carton "greenhouses" These are dandy. You cut the bottom off a milk carton and jam that thing right over the top of your tomato plant. Ta-da! Greenhouse! On cold nights, you screw on the little lid. On warm days, you take the lid off. Then once evenings warm up, you put the lids on all of them and stack 'em in the garage until next year.

Miniature hoophouse

This is basically a miniature hoop house that's from one to three feet tall, depending on how tall you want it to be. You take some PVC tubing out to the garden, hoop it every couple of feet, then place plastic sheeting over the hoops. During cold weather, or at night, you close the ends; on warm days you open them. The cat will probably take up residence in here. Cats can be jerks sometimes. This is a super way to warm up the soil and extend the season. If you really want to keep the tomatoes warm and extend the season, you can set this up earlier to warm up the soil, plant the tomatoes inside, and then cover them with a sheet inside the hoophouse on very cold nights.

A small hobby greenhouse

The same idea as a miniature hoophouse, only as a semi-permanent structure.

Cold frame

This is good for starting seeds for cole crops and other cool-weather crops. Plant seeds for carrots, radishes, lettuce, spinach, etc., directly in the soil in the cold frame for the earliest crops on the block. You can start tomato plants in here, but they're going to have to be transplanted out eventually, unless you have a really big cold frame.

Floating row covers

These are basically a lightweight fabric that can lie directly on the crops without support, and can provide an extra 2 to 8 degrees of frost protection. These won't keep tomatoes as warm as other methods, but are great for a number of uses around the garden.

Blankets and sheets

The old-fashioned season extenders. Throw them over your crops at night, take them off in the morning.

GROWING TOMATOES IN CONTAINERS

If you have a limited amount of space, or if you have terrible soil, then you can grow your tomatoes in a container. A number of determinate tomato varieties are specially bred for this purpose, bearing a nice bunch of tomatoes in a small pot.

Any tomato variety with the word "Patio" in its name is probably a sure bet. Good varieties include Black Seaman, Patio Princess, Czech's Bush, Sophie's Choice, Silver Fir Tree (also a pretty little tomato plant), Bushsteak (big tomatoes on a little plant), Whippersnapper (its size and yield depend on the size of the container you put it in), Sweetheart on the Patio (cherry tomatoes), Marglobe, Baxter's Bush Cherry, Gardener's Delight (also an heirloom, so you can save the seeds from year to year), Balcony, Bush Early Girl, Stupice, Tumbling Tom Yellow.

Large 20 inch plastic pots with saucers are a good bet for these tomatoes. They're easy to move, store, and sanitize at the end of the season.

Now, the drawback of having a gigantic pot is that it's going to be super-heavy and difficult to move around. But! There are ways you can lighten the load. I used to have large pots of hibiscus trees in my greenhouse, and they were a pain to deal with. Then somebody suggested that I put at the bottom of the pot, to help with drainage and to keep the pot light, Styrofoam packing peanuts. These didn't make my filled pots light as air, but I definitely noticed a difference when I was moving these lighter pots around.

So to set up your container, you can start by putting in a cut-out circle from a window screen at the bottom of the pot. This holds in the soil and materials so you don't get soil and Styrofoam bits coming out when you water. Then you add the Styrofoam peanuts at the bottom, a couple of inches thick. (Be sure you don't get the biodegradable packing peanuts. These will slowly melt away as you keep watering the plant – and you probably don't want to see your tomato plant slowly sinking into the pot as they do!)

Then have a bag of good-quality potting soil handy. Don't use soil out of the garden, as it's very heavy, both in terms of weight and in terms of porosity. A good "soilless" mix is best for your plant. Most potting soils are made from a mix of peat moss, perlite, vermiculite, and other light ingredients that are heavy enough for plant roots to stay moist and for root hairs to grab onto as the root grows into the soil, yet light enough to keep valuable oxygen near the roots without drying them out. (Roots absorb oxygen from the soil to keep the cells in the root alive – and growing! If the soil is too wet, then the roots can't absorb oxygen, and the cells stop "breathing" and die – and so do the roots, which in turn affects the plant badly.)

You can improve the soil in your garden, and you can also improve the soil in your pot. Add a cup of dolomitic limestone to the soil in your pot for calcium and magnesium. You can also add several cups of greensand to the mix. Greensand doesn't get a lot of press, but it's great stuff. It's made from undersea deposits made in the ocean like a million years ago, and is mined in New Jersey, and is high in potassium. Also add a cup of bone meal (calcium and phosphorus) and a cup of blood meal for nitrogen, as well as two cups of kelp meal. Mix it all together. Add your own favorite fertilizer to the mix.

Don't add all the soil to the pot yet, though. Put some soil at the bottom, then set your tomato plant in there, and fill up the pot until only the top five inches is sticking out. Then, as the plant grows, keep adding more soil. This allows you to plant early. You can cover the pots if there's a chance of frost very easily that way. Keep the pots in the warmest place in your yard, and if you really want to plant early, you can lay a sheet of Plexiglas or any transparent plastic over the top and make a miniature greenhouse out of it.

By the way, plant only one plant per pot. This allows it to grow stronger and bear more fruit. If it's competing with another tomato, it's not going to do as well.

As the tomato grows, keep adding soil to fill in around the plant. This helps the tomato develop roots all along its stem, making it sturdy and strong, and also all those roots are absorbing all those nutrients you added to the soil.

Fill the pot up with soil to two inches from the top. Then put in a small cage made of concrete reinforcing wire. If your area is particularly buggy or insect-prone, cover the cage with nylon anti-bug netting, and clip it into place with clothespins. Remove the netting only if you're harvesting tomatoes, adding fertilizers, or pruning. You can even spray for aphids and whiteflies through the netting. Or, if your pests are larger (birds, chipmunks, squirrels, neighbors) wrap the cage up in bird netting, and maybe one of those motion-sensitive sprinklers nearby that will fire streams of water at the offender.

Also add a layer of mulch to the pot to keep the moisture in, to keep roots cool in the summer sun, and to keep little weeds from popping up in the potting soil.

Feed your tomatoes with liquid fertilizer such as fish emulsion, Miracle Gro, compost tea, or whichever fertilizer you prefer, about once a month to keep the plants healthy and the tomatoes.

At the end of the season, when the frost hits and the tomatoes are finished, dump the potting soil into the garden, throw away the Styrofoam peanuts, and clean the pots out and scrub them with a bleach solution to get rid of any insect eggs or diseases that might be harbored there. Then put them in the garage and wait for next spring to start afresh.

LOCATION, LOCATION, LOCATION

There's never any perfect location in gardening. Perfection, whether it's in gardening or in anything else in life, is pretty hard to find. But there are plenty of good locations that just need a little tweaking.

The best place to grow tomatoes will have full sun for six hours a day. Hotter southern locations might need a little afternoon shade to give the tomatoes a bit of relief so they can survive and thrive. A well-drained site with rich, loamy soil is ideal. If you don't have a location with full sun for six hours a day, you might have to trim back some tree branches. If your soil isn't ideal, start adding organic material like compost to it.

Have your planting area ready to go, and have plenty of space between your plants. They look tiny now, but they'll eventually produce vines that are 10 to 14 feet long. THAT'S TEN TO FOURTEEN FEET LONG. Plant them two or three feet apart.

When you plan where you want to put tomatoes (and this also goes for peppers, potatoes, and eggplant, which are in the same family as tomatoes), don't plant them in the same places as last year. Also, don't plant tomatoes where you had peppers, potatoes, or eggplants last year. All three of these plants are in the same family – the Nightshade family – and have the same diseases in common. By rotating planting areas, you avoid a buildup of pests and diseases in the same spot year after year.

That's something to keep in mind when planting other plants, too. For example, when marigolds are planted in the same bed again and again, you start seeing nodes on their roots when you pull them up in the fall. The nodes, which look like large bumps, indicate that nematodes have been building up in the soil. These tiny white worms dig into the roots (which cause nodes) and sap the life of the plants. Swap out the marigolds for a different plant – one that is not susceptible to nematodes – and the nematodes will die off.

Variety is a good thing.

Some folks use marigolds as trap plants for nematodes. They plant them in the garden, give the nematodes time to dig into the roots, then yank them (and the nematodes) out of the soil. Bye-bye buggers!

Plant your tomatoes deep!

This is helpful advice in general. Mr. Green Jeans (from the old TV show *Captain Kangaroo*, for you older folks LIKE ME) used a post-hole digger to plant his tomatoes. You can actually plant up to 2/3 of your tomato plant underground – so, if you have a tomato that's ten inches tall, you can bury all of it and leave three inches sticking out of the soil. Yeah, that's deep!

Obviously you can't do that with … well, just about any other plant. But tomatoes are different, because they will actually set roots all the way up and down their stems.

Planting deeply causes the tomato to root deeply. A deep, well-established rooting system can pull more nutrients out of the soil, and will also be protected from drought, able to pull water from deep in the soil. The deep-rooted plant also stays cooler in the heat, and so it can get through summer more easily, and won't fall over during thunderstorms.

If you aren't able to dig this deep, then lay the tomato plant on its side and plant it sideways. You can also pile up soil around your tomato stem as it grows to increase root mass.

The deep-planted tomatoes will take a little extra time to grow. That's because they're putting their energy into rooting. But once they get all rooted, they'll grow like crazy.

Add good stuff to the soil around your tomato plant.

There are all kinds of soil additives you can add to the soil around your tomato plant. Compost is the best soil additive. You can also add well-crushed eggshells for calcium and a half-cup of Epsom salts for magnesium. Both of these help the tomato to resist blossom-end rot. Banana peels also add phosphorus to the soil if you want to add those! Add a handful of natural fertilizer (I like Bradfield fertilizer a lot) to the soil, too.

Mix them all together, then set your tomato plant deep in the hole, dump all that good soil into the hole around it, and water it deeply – several gallons of water should do the trick. Top-dress the soil (that is, lay on top of the soil) about an inch of good compost all around your tomato plant. Once the weather heats up and the soil warms up, lay down a couple of inches of mulch, whether grass clippings, chopped-up leaves from last fall, hay, straw, or anything else. I put down a layer of newspaper mulch.

Get large metropolitan newspapers that have lots of pages (ask your local library for old newspapers if you don't have them), and lay down the newspaper pages ten thick. Of course, be sure to do this on a calm day. Throw a little mulch on top of the pages as you work, just in case you get a breeze. You can lay these pages right on the top of small annual weeds, and even use them to smother perennial weeds. Once the pages are down, throw a nice, thick layer of mulch over the top of them. The newspapers will gradually break down over the year, but they'll keep the ground cool and are very good at suppressing weeds.

Stagger planting

Buy tomato varieties that ripen at different times. Or, plant one portion of your tomato plants, them plant more three weeks later. This helps you space out your tomato harvest if you're planting determinate varieties only.

You'll also have to plant your tomatoes in a different location every year to keep diseases from building up in the soil, and you have to wait three years before you plant tomatoes in the same place where you've planted tomatoes, potatoes, pepper, or eggplants. All of these are in the Solanaceae (or Nightshade) family, and share diseases between them. They're almost as bad as members of the rose family! Almost.

So keep your garden plans from one year to the next so you can make sure you move your tomato plants around and avoid previous planting locations.

Pruning

Do you see a stem on your tomato that is not bearing flowers or fruit? Pinch it off. Then the tomato can divert energy toward fruits. Also, pinching off the suckers will give you a stronger, bushier plant in general.

What if you plant late?

So things happen, and you can't get everything planted on time. Or, you run across some tomato plants on sale toward the end of the season and realize you have a few open spaces in your garden that could easily be filled by a tomato, or two, or maybe 15. What do you do then?

Look at the tag and see how many days your tomato plant needs to fully mature. A lot of tomato varieties need 100 days to mature, but some take only 50 to 60 days to mature. Sixty days is two months. A quick mental calculation will tell you if your tomato will have time to grow tomatoes to full ripeness before the first frost date.

You can even cut some time off the "planting to maturity" thing by planting large, husky tomato plants that already have fruit on them. The pickings are going to be slim out there, as a lot of box stores and nurseries will be clearing out their inventory in late spring and early summer. So if you see a good tomato on sale, then pounce.

Also, if you can, choose tomato varieties those that are fast-ripening varieties – the tag will tell you how many days you have until harvest.

In this case, though, if you want tomatoes fast, grab the small-fruited varieties – cherry tomatoes, grape tomatoes.

You don't have to wait long for these guys at all before you can start popping tomatoes in your mouth. (That's also why I put these in the ground first in early spring – because I do love fast results!) They're small, but hey, they're tomatoes.

When you get your tomaters home (that's my grandpa talking there), plant them in the warmest place you have. Imagine your yard in winter. After the snow falls, in what spot in your yard does it melt most quickly? Grab a shovel and put your tomatoes right there. Now, there's going to be a problem with that – tomatoes will stop production when the temperatures are above 90 degrees. But that doesn't have to be a problem. Rig a little shade cloth to keep the sun off when the thermometer tops 90 degrees.

You have other ways to improve the tomato harvest as the frost date creeps up on you. For large-fruited tomato varieties, you might cull some of the low-quality fruit off the plant. Then the tomato can divert its energy toward ripening the fruit that remains.

SOIL BUILDING – MAKE YOUR DIRT WORK FOR YOU

One of the most important things a gardener can do is to build up the soil in their gardens. But keep in mind that soil-building is not a one-time operation – it's a process. As humus is devoured by microorganisms, worms, and plants, more organic material must constantly be added in order to keep the soil biomass, and thereby the plants, well-fed and happy. Also, humus makes the soil porous and fluffy, builds a strong soil structure, and releases nutrients in a form that's easily absorbed by plant roots.

Chemical fertilizers will not add humus to the soil. These are merely nutritional supplements; plants and their soil need real food – organic material.

But so much good organic material never makes it back into the soil. Leaves, grass clippings, and yard waste ends up choking our landfills instead of nourishing the ground. This is wrong.

Mulch the world!

I have a fairly simple way to deal with weeds: mulch. I like to take newspapers, ten pages at a time, and lay them over the garden, making sure there's enough overlap between each section so light won't get down to the soil. Then I throw straw, grass clippings, leafmould, or whatever on top to make it all tidy and neat.

The neat thing with the newspapers is that you can get a ton of them for your purposes for free, simply by asking your neighbors or by picking them up at the local library. Also, you can lay these newspapers right over the weeds and you never hear another peep out of them for the rest of the year. Even when you have tall grass or weeds up to a foot tall, stomp them down, or mow them, before putting the newspapers on top. They get smothered right out.

The newspapers will also break down and add valuable organic material to the soil. You can lay your tomatoes right on top. You won't have to wipe the dirt off your low-hanging fruits any more. Nice, huh?

Use those leaves

Next, use leaves and excess grass clippings in the garden. Fifteen big bags of leaves, when chewed up by a lawnmower, turn into an inch of mulch on a 15 by 25' garden. (The job took about 30 or 45 minutes.) I did that last fall; this spring, I'm finding worm castings all over!

Pour the leaves out on your garden, mow them into little pieces, and till them under. Or just leave them on top of the soil and don't bother tilling. With mulch, you don't have to worry about your garden drying out – or weeds coming up.

If you don't have leaves, take a trip to the local landfill and get some. There's usually a separate area for yard waste, and there the leaves are free for the taking. (Be careful with grass clippings, because they sometimes contain herbicides. Also, avoid clippings from yards that are treated, as these will contain harmful chemicals as well.) Or grab bags of leaves off the curb before the garbage truck arrives. Or get them from your neighbors; they're always glad to have them taken off their hands.

A note: Don't use leaves if you have a black walnut tree. These leaves contain a chemical that is toxic to tomatoes and other members of the nightshade family, and also suppresses the growth of other plants. (This is a reason why you should not plant a garden near a black walnut tree – because the roots of the tree also contain the same chemical, and your garden will not prosper as a result!)

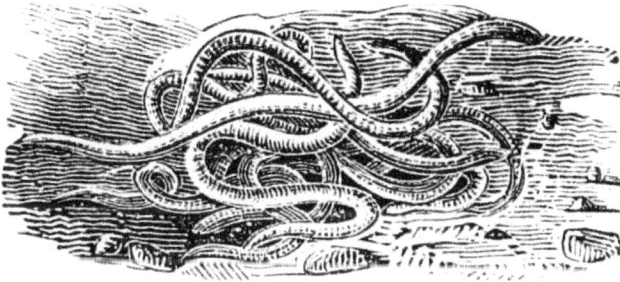

Earthworms = earth movers

The more I read about earthworms and observe them, the more I am convinced that these creatures are a blessing to the soil. They bring up valuable nutrients from the subsoil, their castings are among the best plant food, their tunnels bring air (which is rich in nitrogen) into the ground. Plant roots even seek out earthworm burrows for the nutrients they contain.

Nightcrawlers are best for this work. The red worms, or red wrigglers, prefer to live in compost and leafmould; they're good for mixing up cool compost piles but will not dig very far into the soil. Nightcrawlers will dig burrows deep into the ground, which is what you want.

After it rains, pick earthworms off the sidewalks to put in the garden. Or, go to the bait shop and get them there. See if they'll throw in some egg cases with your worm purchase, because if all the worms don't survive, the egg cases will. Dump a couple of worms out in various places around the garden and cover them with a little soil so they can get underground before the sun and wind dries them out. They generally will get underground within the hour, even on really cold days.

I generally put worms out in the garden every spring. Twelve to 24 worms would probably be good for a small garden, twice that for big gardens.

Green manures

Green manures such as buckwheat, clovers, lespedeza, or oats can be grown between rows, under tall plants, or at season's end all over the garden. In any case, they're tilled under three weeks before a new crop is seeded to allow them to decompose. It's a valuable way to get fast organic material.

Use green manures fill in where a crop has just finished. For example, once the spinach is all picked, throw down some rye seeds or white clover to fill the area in until next spring. Chickpeas make a nice cover crop, and they're edible, and they add much-needed nitrogen to the soil. Daikon radishes are good, too.

Grow legumes as an understory to your hungry corn crop. Leave enough space between the corn rows in order to run a lawnmower between the rows. This will keep the cover crop nice, neat, and low, and the clippings will provide lots of nitrogen-rich mulch for the rest of the garden.

Alfalfa is great for walkways because its clippings, as they break down, release a chemical called triacontanol that acts as a growth stimulant to plants. A small amount of alfalfa clippings can increase vegetable yields by 30 to 60 percent. And those alfalfa roots go deep into the subsoil, pulling up nutrients from deep underground, breaking up soil, and fixing nitrogen.

If you don't want to plant alfalfa, but you want its benefits, you can purchase alfalfa meal at feed stores or order it online. Scatter it over the soil according to package directions to improve growth. Don't spread it too heavily because it will mat and shed water.

Compost

Compost is a fine way to recycle kitchen and garden scraps into fertilizer. And it's earthworm heaven.

Kitchen scraps that are good for compost include such things as fruit and vegetable remains, eggshells, and bread. It's not a good idea to put meat products or leftover milk products in a compost pile (unless it's a very hot pile) due to the possibilities of it attracting dogs and cats. Also it could smell bad. However, if you've been fishing, you can bury the fish bits in the soil. Fish bits are high in nitrogen, and they will make your corn plants love you.

I generally throw my compostables onto the garden during the winter, and put them on the compost pile during the rest of the year. I've heard that compostables on the ground attract mice. But in deep winter they'll also attract songbirds, which is nice. (It's always fun to throw popcorn out to see what kinds of birds I get.)

Some people also dig small holes into particularly infertile areas of the garden, drop compostables into it until it's nearly full, then close it up and start a new one. This doesn't work so well in desert soils – produce buried in sandy soils has been dug up a month later, looking just as fresh as it did when it had been buried.

My soil is evil!

Sometimes you get soil that has basically been created by Satan. Examples of evil soil include subdivision soil – that pasty clay that's created by heavy equipment churning up soil, wet or dry, and compacting it into concrete. Or you have desert asphalt, or fragipan, or stuff you have to take a jackhammer to.

Raised beds are always a good idea here. Lay a thick layer of newspapers over the ground, make an enclosure, then it fill up with compost, rotted manure, and topsoil brought in from elsewhere. Go heavy on the compost! Grow a hedge of deep-rooted legumes around the outside of the enclosure, and underplant tall vegetables (like corn) with small legumes such as white clover. Release nightcrawlers into the soil. This will give you a place to plant while you wait for the compost and the earthworms to do their work on the soil underneath.

Every year, try to mix the good soil in just a little bit more by working a garden fork into the bad soil to aerate it. Keep laying down the organic material. Here, more than anything else, soilbuilding is a process. It will take several years of hard work to bring a dead soil back to life, so be patient.

But a living soil is the best soil for all. So keep at it.

So, keep adding humus in every way, shape, and form you can think of to keep the garden happy and to keep the soil biomass active. This will make an incredible difference in your garden – one you'll definitely love.

STAKING, CAGING, PROPPING THEM UP

Staking!

Indeterminate tomatoes will need this – and even the neat and compact determinates will benefit from staking.

When you first transplant the indeterminate tomatoes outside, stick a 6-foot stake in the ground next to them, deep enough so it won't fall over later in the season.

Let the tomatoes grow without their stake until they form their first flowers. That allows the tomato plants to develop strong stems. Then tie the stem to the stake and prune off the suckers below the first fruits. Suckers are the new stems that form between the leaf and the main stem.

Tie the tomatoes to the stake as they grow. They'll need to be checked often, and tied gently to the stake. The ties must be secure enough to hold the weight of the tomatoes, but not so tightly that you damage the plant. Tie the leader (that is, the growing tip of the plant) very loosely to the stake. To support the fruit as it grows, loop a soft rope or tie above the fruit cluster, then tie it to the stake about six to 10 inches above. Make your tie tight on the stake so the tomatoes won't slide it down with their weight. Tomatoes will grow best this way if they are pruned to a single stem.

As they grow, remove the suckers – the branches that form where the leaf meets the stem – when the suckers are about an inch or two long. Pruning off all the suckers is good for the tomato plant. The sugar in the plant now goes to the fruit, instead of to the suckers, because a pruned tomato plant has only one growing tip (apical meristem in scientific terms – this is the place where the plant produces its growth). When the plant has more than one growing tip going, then the sugar is diverted to plant growth instead of fruit growth.

The other benefit to having a staked tomato grown this way is that fruit production is continuous. The fruits are slightly smaller, but sweeter, and the vine keeps producing late into the season. The leaves all receive sunlight and photosynthesize more effectively. And, finally, it is much, much easier to walk through a garden with staked tomatoes than it is to tiptoe through a sea of tomato vines. So, there is that.

Caging!

Tomato cages are going to be necessary unless you want to give your whole garden over to tomatoes vining everywhere. (This is certainly acceptable if you have the space and don't mind tiptoeing through tomato vines all the time.) I don't know why they sell those tiny little tomato cages that are only three feet tall. Perhaps for the miniature tomato plants? Except there are none? Actually, determinate tomato plants, which bear tomatoes at the top of the plant and stop growing, would work in these smaller cages just fine. For all the rest of your indeterminate tomato plants, if you can get a nice four or five foot tall circle of animal fencing or concrete reinforcing wire, you're in business. If your tomatoes are real monsters, drive a stake or two up against the fencing to support it and zip-tie them together. This will also help keep your cage from falling over due to overloaded plants or stormy winds.

A great way to make super-sturdy cages is to use concrete reinforcing wire. You can buy a roll that's 5 feet tall and 100 feet long. The wire will turn rusty outside, but that doesn't matter – even if it's rusty, the wire cages will last for years.

You'll need a good-quality wire cutter in order to cut sections of the roll off to use as tomato cages. Also, as you're cutting, you will need a helper to stand on the wire while you cut it, or use concrete blocks to hold the wire down. Either way, be careful, as the wire can spring up and could gouge you. This a job for tough gals.

Once you are done cutting the wire, cut off the bottom ring of wire on your tomato cage. This allows you to jab it into the soil around the plant. Success!

Anchor the cage firmly with a steel T-post. You can extend your growing season in early spring or late fall by wrapping each cage with plastic or row covers to make mini-hothouses out of them.

Propping them up!

You can also grow tomatoes up a fence, if it's the right kind of fence. Rigid metal livestock panels typically come in 16-foot lengths, though if you have a hacksaw or something that can cut through wire that's this thick, you can create different sizes. Attach these panels to steel T-posts and then grow the tomatoes up the panels. Or, as reader D. Taylor, did, you can set the fence panels on 10 concrete blocks standing on end. "The plants grow up through the openings in the fence and stay more or less upright until fruit are set when they begin to droop."

Any kind of flat fence that has laterals thin enough to tie the tomato to will do the trick.

A ROGUE'S GALLERY OF GARDEN PESTS

Whiteflies

You'll usually find these tiny, white flies on the undersides of the leaves, and they'll fly up when the leaves are disturbed. The whitefly life cycle is egg, nymphs, pupa, and adult. The immature whitefly nymphs don't have wings and are called crawlers, and actually look more like odd, white leaf spots on the bottoms of the leaves. They don't move much. The whiteflies use piercing-sucking mouthparts to suck the juices out of the plant leaf. In some places, they can spread the virus that causes tomato yellow leaf curl.

Whiteflies usually show up when the plant is stressed, usually when it's too dry.

Whiteflies on a leaf

Insecticidal soap and neem oil plus azadirachtin are good controls. Spray all these on the undersides of the leaves every three days until no more whiteflies are present. Evening sprayings are most effective.

Whiteflies are deucedly hard to get rid of, as the adults scatter as soon as you hit them with a spray. A second tactic that will help is to bring in a handheld vacuum and suck them up all around the plant as they fly up. If you double-team them with several different means of control, you'll have better luck in controlling those little jerks.

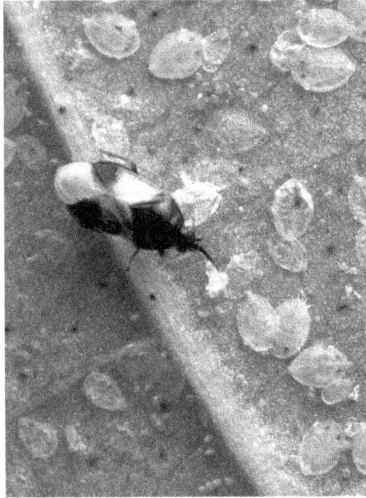

Pirate bugs also help by eating whitefly larvae.

Bring hummingbirds into the garden, as these little birds also eat whiteflies. It couldn't hurt!

Set out yellow index cards covered with petroleum jelly to catch whiteflies. This is supposed to monitor their presence in the garden, but anything that will catch and kill them is tops in my book.

Flea Beetles

These are tiny beetles, a little bigger than actual fleas, but they also jump – hence the name. They multiply like crazy on tomatoes as well as eggplants and other plants, chewing small holes in the leaves, and in no time at all the plant is riddled with holes. Flea beetles can also defoliate and kill plants when they really get out of hand.

The flea beetles overwinter in the soil or garden debris, and when spring warms them up, they come out and eat new growth on their host plants. In late spring or early summer, they lay tiny white eggs in the cracks of the soil around the plants, and the tiny white larvae feed on plant roots. After the larvae pupates, the beetles emerge and head right up into your plant.

Flea beetles overwhelm the plant (and the gardener) through sheer numbers. But as with any insect pest, if you fight the war on several fronts, you will be victorious.

Blasting the plant with water will knock them off the leaves. Follow this up with an application of neem oil or Azatrol EC, which contains the key insecticidal ingredient in neem oil – kind of a pumped-up version. Insecticidal soap also works, as well as kaolin clay, which is sold as Surround WP. The watered-down clay coats the plant while allowing the plant to respire and photosynthesize – actually, this stuff seems to enhance photosynthesis – and keeps the beetles off without harming the helpful insects you need in your garden.

One control method that occurred to me while reading about the life cycle of the flea beetle is this: clear away the mulch around the plant and put black plastic around the plant. Tuck it in tight around the stem and overlap the seams, to keep the beetles from laying eggs, and to prevent the newly-hatched adults from getting out of the soil and onto your plant. I am ordinarily very much for mulch. But if flea beetles have been a problem in your garden for a while, this might cut down their numbers enough so your other control measures have a chance to work.

Another control method is to put floating row covers over your plants to keep the adults from migrating onto your plants. This should keep the damage down and help your additional control methods as well. (Since these are beetles, they can fly in – as well as jump.)

One additional note: A great way to control insect outbreaks is to understand the life cycle of the insect you're trying to stop. By looking at their life cycle, you can find ways to disrupt the insect's breeding or growth. So you can look at the flea beetle's life cycle and think, "So if the larvae is in the soil, I can drench the surface of the soil with soapy water every two weeks and kill them off while they're still underground," which is also an option if you don't have any black plastic. So you upend a bucket of soapy water on the plant every two weeks, making sure you get the leaves and also soak the ground around the plant, making it a two-fer.

Time and again, I've been able to use this understanding to stop insect outbreaks in their tracks, though it helps that I took Dr. Johanna Fairchild's Entomology class in college. *tips hat*

Spider Mites

Hot and dry weather can lead to a spider mite infestation. Tomato plants infested with spider mites generally turn a brownish-red, the leaves looking as if the sun burned them, or the leaves might look yellowish with green veins. When you turn the leaf over, you may see little webs and some tiny salt-and-pepper grit.

Marigolds infested with spider mites tend to turn whitish in the leaves. In advanced cases, the plant becomes swathed in webs until it turns into a marigold mummy.

Control spider mites with a strong spray from a garden hose from underneath. This disrupts their activity and washes off the dust that hides the mites from natural predators.

Another way is to spray horticultural oil, or dormant oil, on the affected plant. This suffocates the mites with a thin layer of oil that still allows the plants to breathe. It's also a safe way to kill the mites, as opposed to chemicals. If you spray horticultural or dormant oil, do it when it's cool, to try and keep the leaves from burning.

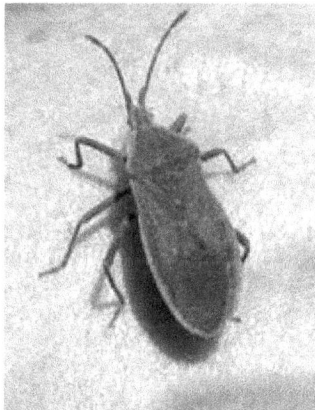

Stink Bugs

This was a surprise to me, as stink bugs had never been a problem in the garden when I was horticulturing back in the day. Apparently they have made up for lost time.

Stink bugs are about the size of a fingernail, but they're green or brown and can blend in very well with the plant or ground. I knew them from when I was young, when I'd sit down in the leaves while walking in the woods, and when I would stir up the leaves, sometimes I'd smell this pungent odor from the stink bugs I disturbed in the leaves. The smell is much, much worse if you put your hand in the leaves and accidentally squish one.

What kind of damage does a stink bug do?

Stink bugs stick their piercing-sucking mouthparts under the tomato's skin and inject an enzyme that liquefies the tomato at that particular spot. Then they suck up the tomato liquid. These bugs (they are actually true bugs) leave dark pinprick spots on the tomato, or odd knots. The damage I recognized, however, was a light stippling on the fruit's surface. I've seen that on my own tomatoes, and didn't know what caused it until now. One mystery solved.

They also dive-bomb you, just for kicks apparently.

But a stink bug infestation can cause severe damage to the fruits. When you have a lot of stink bugs sticking their mouthparts into your tomatoes, now and then you'll get a mouthpart that has some yeast on it from heaven knows where. Once the yeast (or some other microbe) gets inside the tomato, the fruit is further infected.

Predatory insects, like ladybugs, assassin bugs, and wheelbugs will attack stink bugs. Chickens may be helpful in controlling them (I have a few hens that I let wander through the garden and haven't seen any stink bug damage – this is not a scientific analysis, naturally).

Squishing them (if you can put up with the stink), dumping them in a bucket of soapy water, and spot-spraying infestations are control methods. Use several control methods at the same time – this usually brings home the bacon.

Tomato Hornworms

These are gigantic green caterpillars, ranging from about the size of your little finger to the size of a pickup truck – well, maybe not that big, but close enough – that will eat your tomato leaves to skinny, stunted skeletons and drop big caterpillar poop everywhere. They are ugly as sin. I generally will squash any insect between my fingers, but I will not squash these. I don't like to step on them, either, as they pack an incredible amount of green goo in their innards. Some people say that chickens like them. This may or may not be true. I used to offer these to the geese and ducks at the city rose garden, and they wanted nothing to do with hornworms. When I found these on my nicotiana plants, I'd grab them and heave them as hard as I could toward the lagoon, watching with satisfaction as that damn caterpillar soared like a bird toward the water and the rocks.

Handpicking these caterpillars is the best way to go. You would think these would be pretty easy to find, but they can be deceptively plant-like, even for their enormous size. If you notice some of your tomato leaves have suddenly been defoliated, immediately look for caterpillar poop. If you see some, go straight up on the plant above it until you find the caterpillar from whence it came. Then drop the caterpillars in a bucket of soapy water.

However, if you see a caterpillar that has little white things sticking out of it, it's been filled with parasites. Leave those in your garden to spread the caterpillar parasites and help with natural control.

These guys are walking intestinal tracts (any caterpillars are), so they'll leave evidence of the evil they're doing.

After the tomatoes are done, till the soil to expose and kill burrowing caterpillars and pupae.

The adult form of these caterpillars is the sphinx moth, a large, brown-winged moth. I like these moths, and you see them at twilight, humming in front of the petunias and sipping from the blossoms. But I have no love for the tomato hornworm.

Ants farming aphids on plant roots.

Aphids

Aphids are small bugs, but they can pack a wallop because they reproduce so quickly and can take over your plants fast. Aphids, sometimes called plant lice, are tiny sap-sucking insects that appear on soft stems and new foliage. Generally they are green but sometimes you'll see black or wooly white aphids. You'll see little white specks on your tomato leaves, which turn out to be tiny bugs, and then you turn the leaf over and you'll see that you have a lot more where that came from.

Aphids reproduce by laying eggs AND through giving live birth AND they don't need to sexually reproduce because females can create baby aphids on their own! Great news, right? or not.

Yet the green, pear-shaped bugs have no exoskeleton to protect them from predators, and any ladybug or lacewing can find them and eat them up.

So how do aphids survive so successfully?

The answer: Ants protect them. When you stroke an aphid's back, the aphid secretes honeydew – that is, they put out a little drop of sugar. Ants have figured this out, so

42

when the ants discover that aphids have taken over a plant, the ants will organize and protect the aphids. The ants stroke the aphids' backs to get honeydew, then take the honeydew back to the anthill. Ants "farm" aphids the way a farmer raises dairy cattle. Some species of ants will even carry aphid eggs back to the anthill in fall so the eggs have a safe, warm place to hatch, then put the newly-hatched aphids back onto the plants in spring. Ants even pick up aphids in their mandibles and carry them around (unlike humans and their cows).

Under the ants' protection, aphid thrive, sipping plant juices through their piercing-sucking mouthparts and leaving honeydew all over the leaves of the host plant, which causes sooty mold fungus to attack the plant.

Ants will even fight for possession of the aphids. When aphids took up residence on my "Autumn Joy" sedum, two tribes of ants – one red, one black – claimed them, and went to war on the plants. Ants kept grabbing other ants to hurl them off the plant.

The best way to deal with a situation like this – well, besides sitting down and watching the show – is to get the plant away from the ants, rob the aphids of protection, and allow natural predators to help you finish off the aphids.

I poured soapy water over the sedum, rubbing the leaves and stems to get all the aphids I could. A few drops of soap per gallon works just fine, and you can rinse the plant off with clear water afterward. Once the aphids were gone, the ant battles ceased – on that plant, anyway, since I didn't really keep track of the ants and their wars after that.

Once the ants are gone, you can discourage aphids. A good blast of water will knock them off the plant. You can dust the plant with diatomaceous earth (also called DE). This is made up of microscopic diatoms, just like a piece of chalk, and the diatoms are sharp-edged, cutting through an insect's protective waxy layer (called chitin), which causes the insect to dry up and die. Diatoms is why a slug will explode if it crawls over a chalk line on the sidewalk. DE works well against any insect, good or bad, so be careful to keep this out of flowers when you're dusting the plant with it. Also wear a dust mask and gloves when applying it, as it will also cut up your breathing passages if you inhale too much of it.

Insecticidal soap, neem oil, kaolin clay, or a bucket of soapy water (not detergent), will all help.

If you fertilize regularly, cut back on the nitrogen. This element, which plants use to produce new growth, also makes the leaves soft and juicy for insect pests. Insects will jump on a succulent plant the way you'd jump on a juicy steak (or a sweet, juicy apple if you're a vegetarian).

For some reason, aphids prefer some varieties of tomatoes while they leave others alone. It's possible some tomato varieties taste better to aphids than others. We'll just file this under "Insects Are Weird, case number 2,234,983,023,809."

Kaolin Clay for Pest Control

One effective control against stink bugs, flea beetles and most other bugs is kaolin clay. This is a new one on me but it looks very helpful.

Kaolin is a type of clay often used in kitty litter (if I'm remembering my Soils class correctly). But when it's finely ground and combined with water in a 1 to 6 percent concentration, it's been proven to act as an effective barrier to pests, and also acts as protection from the worst of the sun. The reflective white film that kaolin forms over the leaves actually helps photosynthesis while reducing heat stress. It's used in orchard production, and can be effective in the home garden to repel insects such as stink bugs and many other plant-eating insects. Be sure to completely cover both surfaces of the leaf when spraying this, both upper and lower.

Now in one study, when kaolin clay was used on cotton plants, an aphid infestation actually got worse. So as with any preventative measure, it's not perfect. But this sounds like a really helpful option. Try it out with your other pest-control measures, and see what kinds of results you get.

DISEASES AND GENERAL AFFLICTIONS

The Mysterious Letters On the Tag

When buying tomatoes, look for the letters A, F, V, T, or N on the tag. These tell you what diseases this particular tomato variety is resistant to.

An "A" means it's resistant to Alternaria stem canker. An "F" or "V" shows resistance to Fusarium or Verticillium wilt. "T" means the tomato is resistant to tobacco mosaic virus. (Incidentally, cigarettes can bring this disease into the garden soil, through the tobacco in the cigarette. Even the cigarette ash can spread the virus, which is not destroyed by that little fire from your match.) Finally, an "N" means it's resistant to nematodes, tiny white roundworms that burrow into the roots. Plant tomatoes as deeply as you can. Roots will form along the stem that's underground. That will give you a deep-rooted plant that will withstand drought.

I have included as many of the mysterious letters as I could find. If you've had trouble with various forms of blight in the past, or odd diseases that you haven't been able to identify, pick up some tomatoes with extra letters and see if those help.

A – The tomato is resistant to Alternaria leaf spot and stem canker.

EB – Early blight

F – The tomato is resistant to Fusarium wilt. However, the disease has evolved, so these old F tomatoes might not be resistant to the new strains of the disease.

FF - Race 1 & Race 2 Fusarium – These tomatoes are resistant to the second generation of Fusarium.

FFF - Fusarium, Races 1, 2, and 3 – These tomatoes are all up to date on their Fusarium resistance – until a new strain comes along! Because it will.

L - Septoria leaf spot

LB – Late blight, also known as water mold

N - Nematodes

T - Tobacco mosaic virus

V - Verticillium wilt

St - Stemphylium (Gray Leaf Spot)

TSWV - Tomato Spotted Wilt Virus

Sunscald

This usually occurs when tomato plants have lost a lot of leaves and the tomatoes are exposed to the direct rays of the hot sun. (This is common on pepper plants as well – as they are in the same family as tomatoes.) Usually sunscald takes place on plants that were previously shaded or leafy but suddenly were exposed to the sun.

If for some reason your tomato plant is suddenly exposed to the sun, drape a lightweight material over the fruit during the brightest part of the day to minimize exposure. Try to keep leaf diseases at bay as much as possible – though sometimes stuff happens, as we all know. Seek out tomatoes that are resistant to Septoria leaf spot and early blight. (But then again, if your tomato catches early blight, it's pretty much hosed – and sunscald will be the least of your worries as your tomato plant is pretty much doomed.

A nice dose of nitrogen once the fruits have set will help guard against sunscald.

Pick sunscalded fruits if they're close to getting ripe and let them ripen inside. A sunscalded tomato is still edible – just cut it off before you eat the tomato. Don't let black mold start on the sunscalded part, or then the tomato will go bad.

Typical leaves with tobacco mosaic

Tobacco Mosaic

If your plants had tobacco mosaic, burning or composting the leaves will not kill the virus, because the viruses can survive incredible temperatures. That is why you shouldn't crush out a cigarette in your garden.

If a tobacco plant infected with the virus got into that cigarette, its ashes will pass the virus on to your roses and other plants, especially plants in the nightshade family, such as potatoes and tomatoes. So don't smoke in the garden, or at least don't tap out your cigarette ashes in the garden, and don't put cigarettes in the compost or your soil.

If a tomato plant develops the crazed leaves of tobacco mosaic virus, pull it up and throw it out of the garden. Don't compost it – just throw it away. Don't plant any member of the Solanaceae family there – no eggplants, tomatoes, potatoes, peppers, or Nicotiana flowers – as the disease will affect any member of this family.

Blossom End Rot

This might be a problem on tomatoes (and also peppers) if the soil moisture has been uneven. This disease will also come back year after year. It is due to a lack of calcium in the soil, and shows up as a black spot on the blossom end that grows bigger and blacker and uglier – the black spot is from a fungus that attacks the weakened fruit.

The kicker is that it's possible to have a lot of calcium in the soil, but an alkaline soil (pH of 8 and up) can "tie up" the calcium – that is, the high alkalinity of the soil creates a tighter bond between the soil particle and the calcium, and so the plant root is unable to pick that calcium off or take it for itself.

TL;DR – If blossom end rot is a recurring problem, get a soil testing kit from your local University Extension service and find out what is wrong with your soil. Do this in fall, or even in summer. That way, you'll have plenty of time to find out what your soil needs, and then you can keep blending in the proper amendments, keep adding compost, keep adding good organic mulch. You'll also be shown how to maintain the soil's pH to a more favorable level. Maybe by spring your soil will be in better shape and ready to release calcium (and every other nutrient) like crazy.

Another difficulty is when you get a lot of drought, then a lot of heavy rainfall. This is why it's so helpful to water your plant consistently every week (if needed) or even twice a week if it's especially dry. Keeping the soil evenly moist helps keep the disease at bay.

When you notice blossom-end rot starting on your tomatoes, however, you do have some short-term fixes available. You can actually water several antacid tablets into the soil around your tomato plants, which will make calcium readily available. (Use antacids that don't have aluminum for best results.) Or give your tomatoes a foliar feeding of any fertilizer that has calcium as one of the minerals. Water the leaves and roots for best results.

Tomatoes with Late Blight

Potato Blight, Late Blight, and Early Blight

Last year my Celebrity tomatoes developed dark blotches when the tomatoes were still very small and green. Each time the blotches quickly spread over the whole fruit and turned it into brown mush. I was aggravated. I had one tomato that I thought had finally made it to maturity, but when I picked it up, I found it had been half-eaten by this rot.

This wasn't limited to the tomatoes touching the ground, either; tomatoes up in the air were also getting these blotches. And, even stranger, the tomatoes on the other side of the garden were doing just fine – no weird blotches. What was going on?!

My tomato had late blight, the same disease that caused the great potato famine in Ireland. (Potatoes and tomatoes are in the same plant family, the Solanaceae, aka the Nightshade family, which means they share many diseases.) It develops in wet, humid, cool conditions – the kind of weather that my tomato plants had been experiencing. When you have a blighted tomato, one side of the fruit may look lovely, but the other side is slimy, rotted away, and brownish-black.

Tomato stem with late blight.

Late blight (also known as potato blight) is caused by *Phytophthora infestans*, an oomycete (a fungus-like microorganism). There are many different varieties and forms of blight, including anthracnose fruit rot (which makes bulls-eye shaped circles on tomatoes), **early blight** (where the petal ends on the tomatoes turn white with fungus), and **Septoria leaf spot** (which affects only leaves and stems, leaving them peppered with little black spots).

The leaves on plants affected by blight have little brown spots on them, as if a few drops of acid fell on them. On the back of the leaves, or on their tops, is a lot of white, powdery mold.

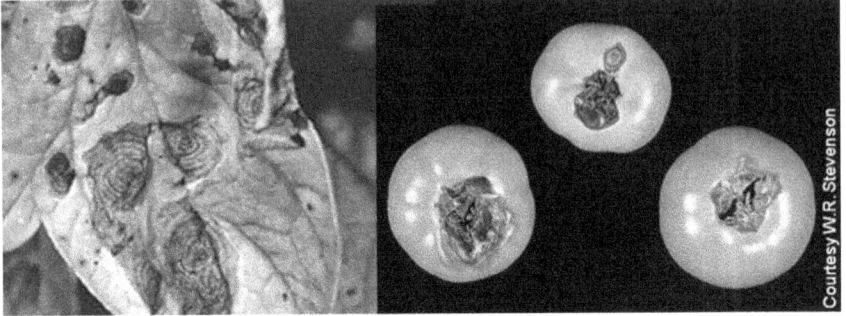

Tomatoes with early blight
Courtesy of Utah State University Extension

It should be noted that in some places, the fungus has developed resistance to systemic fungicides. However, external fungicides – those that repel fungus by changing the pH of the outside of the plant – still do the trick *if you start spraying them immediately after you plant your tomatoes and potatoes.* Keep spraying the fungicide weekly (or as often as the label specifies).

The drawback is that the fungicide will have to be reapplied every time it rains. Also, by the time blight has appeared on your tomatoes, it will be too late for a fungicide to do any good. Fungicide can be used only as a *preventative* measure, not a cure.

However, some experts are not sure how much good spraying actually does, so you might take notes about your spraying program. See what works and what doesn't.

One way of outsmarting the disease may be to plant a wide variety of disease-resistant tomato plants, not just one variety. Even if you lose one or two tomato plant to the disease, the other varieties could resist it. Also, space the tomato plants well apart from each other. My tomato plants were scattered around the garden, well apart from each other, and this probably saved some of my plants.

Mulch the potatoes and tomatoes to avoid water splash-up from the soil. Sometimes blight spores are splashed up onto the plant from the bare soil. Also, water early in the day so the plant has time to dry off before nightfall. Don't plant tomatoes where you had any potatoes, tomatoes, eggplants, or peppers the previous year. This can be tough if you have a small garden and not much room to move things around. Do your best.

Give potato and tomato plants plenty of space in the garden for good air circulation. You might trim off parts of your tomato plant, especially if it's a monster plant, to let the air travel through.

As soon as you see infected fruits or foliage, remove them and burn them. (Don't compost them unless your pile gets really, really hot.) Bag them up and get them out of the garden so no more fungus spores can spread. (Spores come out of the fruiting bodies in the brown spots.)

Some tomato plants, such as Mountain Fresh, Mountain Supreme, and Plum Dandy, show resistance to the disease. Look specifically for these kinds of tomatoes if you've had blight in the past.

When you fertilize, keep the nitrogen levels low. Nitrogen makes leaves juicier and more succulent for diseases. Don't save seeds from infected crops, since the disease can be spread through the seeds.

If blight gets out of control, you'll have to pull up and destroy any infected plants as soon as you see them. Keep spraying fungicide on the survivors.

If you had trouble with late blight in your garden last year, take preventative measures by spraying those vegetables with Bordeaux mixture every two weeks during hot and humid weather. Copper fungicides will also work against this disease. It helps if you pick off the affected leaves, too, and dispose of them away from the garden (not in the compost heap!). Don't allow volunteer potatoes or tomatoes to grow in your garden.

EARLY MICHIGAN TOMATO.

Fusarium Wilt

Fusarium wilt is a fungus that attacks tomato plants, as well as squash and melon plants. Fusarium starts in the roots and moves from there into the stems. If your plant is hardly growing and is all stunted, that's probably what the problem is. Then they wilt and die. Sometimes a white fungus starts growing on the dead vines.

If this happens, get the dead vines out of the garden ASAP so the spores don't spread back into the garden. Don't plant any melons or tomatoes there next year, or the next, because Fusarium will linger in the soil. Your best bet is to plant resistant varieties.

Heat Will Stop Tomato Production

When the heat is particularly intense, plants will stop producing. Tomatoes stop production when temperatures soar above 90 degrees. Cucurbits (zucchini, cucumbers, muskmelon) might produce a bunch of male flowers but no female flowers, much to the gardener's frustration. (Unless she has more than enough zucchini.)

Temperatures of 85 to 90 degrees in the day and night temperatures above 75 degrees will also stop tomato flowers from being pollinated, and even cause them to drop off the plant.

Tomatoes on the vine and already close to being ripe will be okay in the heat – but only up to a point. These fruits will be more susceptible to sunscald.

Tomatoes will have a hard time reaching full ripeness in the heat. Fruits that typically ripen as red will turn orange and then be unable to finish ripening. Pick these fruits and bring them inside, out of the sun, so they can finish ripening. This will help ease the energy burden on your tomato plant, too.

However, some heat-tolerant tomatoes will keep producing even in high temperatures. Heatmaster, Solar Fire, Summer Set, Florida 91, Phoenix, and other "heat-set" tomatoes have been bred to bear fruit even when the temperatures soar. Or, you can plant determinate tomatoes, which will bear their fruit and then be all done before the serious heat starts up.

Another alternative is to set up shade cloth to keep the sun off the tomato plants. Set the shade cloth up so the tomatoes will get a good dose of morning sun, and then are shaded from the hot afternoon rays. Use "50 percent" shade cloth, which will reduce sunlight by 50 percent and heat by 25 percent. Then join the tomatoes in the shade with a good book.

Be sure to have a nice, thick layer of mulch over the tomato roots. This will cool the ground and help keep the plant cool. Also, keep watering the plants to help with heat stress.

Keep an eye on diseases. Heat-stressed plants tend to be more susceptible to diseases and insects. So, if you see something coming on, then nip it in the bud.

Reader D. Taylor points out that Baker Creek Seed Company sells a tomato from Iraq called Ninevah, which tolerates heat and drought very well.

THE 3 GREAT MARKET TOMATOES

NONE OTHERS CAN COMPARE

BRANDYWINE LARGEST, HANDSOMEST & MOST PRODUCTIVE

ATLANTIC PRIZE EARLIEST OF ALL

EARLY MARKET CHAMPION FINEST PURPLE VARIETY

HARVESTING TOMATOES

I always love when the first tomato is ripe enough for me to pick it off the vine and pop it in my mouth. (That's one reason I plant cherry tomatoes – because of the very short time to harvest.) Really, a lot of gardeners are fit to bust when they're waiting on that first ripe tomato. Who can blame them? A sun warmed, fully ripe tomato is one of God's treats. Waiting 45 days for a ripe tomato? Not bad. Waiting 100 days for one of those big beefsteak tomatoes? Okay, that's going to be tough!

The nice thing about tomatoes is that you can pick a tomato before it's ripe, and it will keep ripening. However, once a tomato is picked, it no longer draws in oxygen from the mother plant, which affects the formation of sugar. That's why ripened tomatoes are never as sweet as vine-ripened tomatoes. And of course, this is why store tomatoes never taste as good and sweet as a home-ripened one: They are all picked while they're green, for easier shipping, and are then ripened before they go to the store.

A tomato is ripe when it has a deep, rich, even color on the vine, with no green spots. If you gently squeeze it, the tomato is firm but soft at the same time. Squeezing an unripe tomato is like squeezing a golf ball. It will taste like one, too.

As with any living thing, a rule of thumb does not cover all varieties. Some heirlooms will ripen before they completely change color. Cherry tomatoes should be picked just before they're perfectly ripe, as some varieties tend to crack if left too long on the fine.

Of course, the sure-fire way to test for ripeness is to take a bite. The taste test never fails. (Well, unless you accidentally get a slug in your mouth in that first bite and your whole mouth goes numb.)

Tomatoes (and cucumbers too) will keep longer if you leave a short stem on the fruit. Use pruning shears or scissors for best results.

If you have to pick some tomatoes a little before their time, remember that warmth ripens them, not light. If the day is warm but overcast, for instance, they'll still ripen just fine. Don't ripen them in full sun, though.

Wash and dry your tomatoes before storing them.

In the end, the best way to harvest a tomato is to pick it off the vine and pop it directly into your mouth.

Food Pantry Plea

If you're tempted to use the excess zucchini from your garden as baseball bats, or have tomato fights, stop! Take that produce to your local food kitchen or charitable food pantry. Why waste it when someone can taste it? (And they'll thank you for it, too.)

Fresh produce is always in demand, and it's always sweet and good to one who's fallen on hard times. (With as many layoffs we've seen, and as tight as the job market is, you probably even know someone who could use that extra help.)

If you're not sure where your local food kitchen is, ask a pastor or priest. Also, many churches hold food drives that you can participate in.

Getting Tomatoes Ready for Harvest

Gardeners with tomato vines start getting concerned this time of year. They look at all the green tomatoes that are taking their sweet time to ripen, then look at the calendar and see that the first frosts are around the corner.

Help the tomato plant direct its resources toward ripening its fruit. First, tomatoes need about 40 to 50 days after the blossoms set to ripen. If you have fewer than 40 to 50 days to frost, take the blossoms and small fruit off the vines. Also, take off any fruit that's deformed. Keep the best and the most mature tomatoes of the crop, and take off anything else.

Then, prune back any vigorous shoots. Don't take off anything that has a lot of leaves on it, since the plant needs the energy produced in those leaves. Also, try tip pruning. This is where you pinch off the tips of your tomato plants to stop them from growing. The plants then can turn their remaining time before frost toward fruit development.

The Truth About Green Tomatoes

Immature green tomatoes won't ripen off the vine, but mature green tomatoes will. These are just about as large as a red tomato, and are turning from green to white. Store them in open cardboard boxes and give them about two weeks to ripen at 70 degrees.

Eudora Weldon of Graham, Mo., said, "I want to tell you green tomatoes will ripen. Wrap them in newspapers and store them in a cool place in a cardboard box. Check them in a few weeks. We have tomatoes until Christmas."

So you can do that. If you want to use some of your green tomatoes, make relish out of them, or piccalilli, or fry your green tomatoes, just like in the book.

Just don't take your green tomatoes to a theatrical performance, even if it is a bad one....

THE WRONG KIND OF APPLAUSE.

The Cellar

CANNING AND PRESERVING

Keep Tomatoes Available All Winter. Can, freeze, or dry tomatoes from your garden. (Better yet – do all three.)

I prefer to freeze sweet corn whereas tomatoes and green beans are better canned. But I also freeze tomato puree with basil, and add that to winter soups.

Are you new to food preservation? Contact your cooperative extension office in your county for information on classes or bulletins related to food preservation. Be sure to add all of those peelings and rinds to your compost pile.

Canning Tomatoes

Now back in the day, we did this in a hot kitchen and it seemed to take forever and there were tomatoes and tomato bits everywhere, and since I was a kid I wasn't even a fan of tomatoes, though I did like them in spaghetti sauce. I guess things change when you get older and gain, what's that word, perspective? Well at any rate, canning is easier these days, and central air conditioning certainly eases the heat!

Of course, I can't complain – at least my mom wasn't canning on a wood stove. My grandmas, on the other hand, probably did. Good times, people.

Even though I've canned my own stuff since then, and found it relatively easy and didn't even break a sweat doing it, I still associate canning with the old days. I probably should fix that!

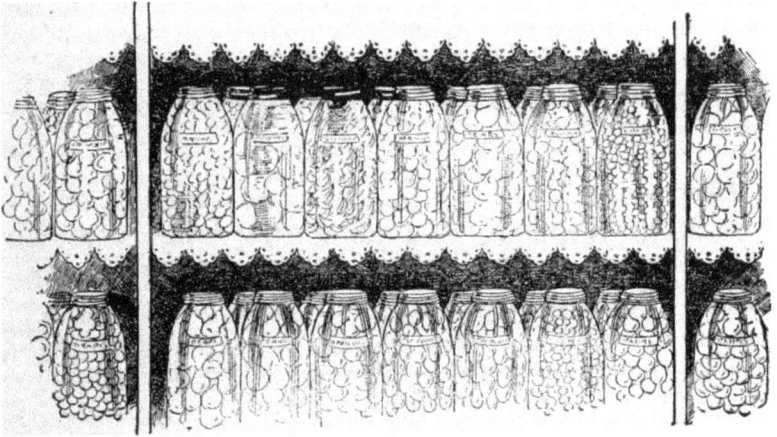

Gather all your supplies

Get out your pressure cooker. If you're reusing jars from last year, check them for chips in the lip of the jar that would keep then from sealing properly, and discard any that do. Then run the jars through the dishwasher to sterilize them properly. Have enough seals and lids on hand for the operation. Also have a couple of extra pot holders ready to deploy if the potholder you're using gets drenched in boiling water.

Get jar grippers and jar lifters, a canning funnel.

Then get your tomatoes prepared. If you want salsa, sauce, whole tomatoes, crushed tomatoes, or halved tomatoes, fix them up the way you like. Sorry to not provide recipes, but "Dammit Jim, I'm a horticulturist, not a sous-chef!" Besides, the recipes you use for your stuff are better for your uses than mine, so there is that.

One note: Whole tomatoes are easier to can, and they also produce more pectin for better canning results.

Be sure to put your lids in boiling water for three to five minutes to sterilize them, then set them aside to dry. Run your jars through the dishwasher to sterilize them, and leave them in there to stay warm. You will need to have your jars warm when you are packing them for best results.

Take the skins off your tomatoes

This is fairly straightforward. Have a big kettle of water boiling on the stove, with a big bowl of ice water nearby. Cut the stem out, and score the bottom of each tomato with an X. Put them in the boiling water for a minute, or two minutes if you have really big tomatoes.

Then use a slotted spoon to remove the tomatoes and put them in the ice water. If you have a blanching basket, you can lower them all at once into the boiling water, lift them out, then set them in the ice water. If you are processing gallons of tomatoes, you might want to go that route.

Then wipe them off and slip off the skins.

Empty out the big pot, fill it with clean water, and get that to boiling if you are using boiling water to pack them.

Packing the tomatoes

Then place your tomatoes in the jars. Be sure to have the jars warm when you're putting the tomatoes in. One way is to run them through the dishwasher just before you start, and leave them in there, ready to go, until you need them. (Don't use dishwashing soap unless you are reusing them.)

Pack the tomatoes in, pressing on them as you go so all the spaces in the jar fill with juice. Leave a head space of a half-inch. Then run a knife around the inside of the jar to get all the air bubbles out.

Add lemon juice. A pint jar needs a tablespoon of lemon juice, and the quart or liter jars will need two tablespoons.

Reader D. Taylor does a cross between hot pack and canning. Boil your tomatoes for 45 minutes, then add ½ tsp. coarse salt per pint, and sometimes you might add 1 tsp. lemon juice per pint as well. This is more of a puree, as the tomatoes are so completely boiled down, but they work great in soups and stews.

Wipe the edges of your jars with a clean towel, to get rid of any tomato bits that would interfere with the seal. Then put your lids on and process them, whether with boiling water or a pressure cooker. Be sure to meet or exceed USDA guidelines, as botulism can occur from improperly canned food, even tomatoes.

Let them stand overnight. The next day, check the seals. All the lids should be sucked in, and none of them should pop up and down. If they do, put them in the fridge and use them within the next few days. Don't try to re-can them. That's just bad news.

Then line up your jars in your pantry or cellar and enjoy.

Freezing Tomatoes

I tend to really like this method the best because it is the easiest method: freezing your tomatoes.

You can actually freeze whole tomatoes – they don't look like much when they thaw, but their skins come right off when they thaw, and you can use them any way you like and they taste great. Wash them off, stick them in a freezer bag, and put them in the freezer. You're done! In winter, you can thaw them out by running them under warm water – and the skins slip right off. Then you let them thaw out, squeeze out the seeds, and put them into your stew or soup. (Shoot, you don't even need to completely thaw them before you put them in your stew or soup. Just put 'em in there.) You don't even need to blanch them beforehand, since the skins slip right off when they're thawed.

I liked to puree my tomatoes in the blender with a couple leaves of basil and a clove or two of garlic. I leave them in their skins and don't do anything to them except to cut them into pieces, squeeze out the seeds, and pop them into the blender and start pureeing. When they're liquefied, I pour them into freezer bags and pop them into the freezer that way. I add these to soups in winter.

I prefer to freeze stuff, because it's easy and for me, easy stuff is so much easier than hard stuff, and then I have more time to do important things like procrastinate from my writing.

EARLY FREEDOM

How to Sun-Dry Tomatoes

So you have a bounty of tomatoes. Sun-dried tomatoes at the store cost an arm and a leg – so make your own with home-grown fruit.

Some people dry them with the skins on, but some prefer to take the skins off before drying. Boil a large pot of water. Using a slotted spoon, slip several tomatoes at a time into the boiling water for 45 seconds to a minute, or up to two minutes for big tomatoes. Then scoop them out, right into a bowl of ice water. The skins will slide right off the tomatoes.

Cut the stem and the hard part under it out of the tomato. Cut the tomato in half (but if it's a big tomato, more than two inches long, cut it in quarters). Scoop out all the seeds, but keep as much of the pulp as possible. Lightly salt the tomatoes. You can also sprinkle on herbs such as basil or oregano. This will really make the house smell nice as you're drying the tomatoes.

Then lay the tomatoes, with the cut surface up, on non-stick cookie sheets, or on a glass container. Don't use aluminum – these will react with the acid in the tomatoes.

Bake for three hours with the oven at 170 degrees, or on the oven's lowest setting, but leave the oven door open three inches. This allows moisture to escape. After three hours, turn the tomatoes over and press them flat with a spatula. Repeat the turning and flattening every three hours until the tomatoes are dry. If you want to speed up the process, you can raise the temperature to 200 degrees for a short while, but you will have to watch them like a hawk.

If you're using a dehydrator, put them on the trays with the cut side up. This time, turn them over and flatten them after 4 to 5 hours, and keep repeating the turning and flattening until they are completely dry.

Sun-drying will take about three days. You'll need a series of very hot days to do this successfully. Place the tomatoes with the cut sides down

You could dry them outside, but something that will work better – and is more dependable – is sun drying them in your car. Put them in shallow trays (because you don't want to have to worry about them leaking juice in your car), put the trays on the dashboard or in the back window of your car, roll up the windows, and park in the full sun. Start in the morning and keep them in there until the sun goes down. Bring the tomatoes into the house overnight. It should take about two days to finish these up.

Dried tomatoes should be flexible, like raisins, and not brittle, and they shouldn't stick to your hands. Let them cool, then stick them in a ziplock bag. You can throw them in the freezer if you like, though you don't have to. A cool, dry place also works.

You can also make fruit leathers with tomatoes. Mush them up or puree them, then spread them out on plastic wrap to ¼ inch thick. If they are gloppy, add a tiny bit of tomato juice to help them pour out. But don't make them too thin or then you'll have to lick them off the plastic, which doesn't work so well. You can oven-dry or sun-dry them. If you use the oven, don't let the heat get over 130 degrees, or you might scorch the fruit leathers or even melt the plastic! When the top part is dry, peel the tomato mixture off the plastic and flip it over and dry the other side. Then roll or stack and keep them in a plastic bag when they're dried.

Storing and using dried tomatoes

Dry the food until it's leathery and dry with no moisture in the middle of the food. After you've dried several batches, you will start to be able to feel whether the slices are dry enough or not. Often, to make the drying process go faster, I'll open up the dehydrator and take out any fruit that's already dry, opening up gaps in the trays to allow more air circulation.

I dehydrate the fruit until it's quite dry, with no hint of moisture on it. My tomatoes turn out crisp.

When the fruit is done, I let it cool off. Then dump the pieces into freezer bags marked with the variety and the date, then let them sit on the counter with the mouth of the bag open just to make sure everything's dry. If I see the tiniest bit of condensation, back to the tray they go. If they stay dry, after a day or two I'll seal the bag and toss it in the freezer. (You can keep the bags in a cool, dry, dark place and they'll be fine, but I like the freezer best.)

You can also store the dried fruit in sealed mason jars as long as you store them in a dark place. Light is bad for dried produce. Don't store dried food in anything metal – but you can put the food in a plastic bag so the dried produce is not touching the metal.

If you want to reconstitute the dried fruit for cooking, soak it for about 12 hours. As far as dried tomatoes go, I love to use them in soup. All I do is throw them into the pot with the rest of my ingredients, then simmer them nicely for 30 minutes, and they come out tasting just fine.

For more information: Your local university extension service is a wellspring of good information, and they will give you bulletin after bulletin about drying food, and indeed anything else, if you just ask politely. I also love *The Encyclopedia of Country Living* by Carla Emery, which offers the lowdown on drying as well as just about any other aspect of good old-fashioned food production, from vegetable planting to canning to setting up a poultry flock to milk handling and cheese recipes. Lots of good stuff.

One ounce will produce about thirteen hundred plants.

How To Save Seeds From Tomatoes

In fall, you can save seed from favorite open-pollinated tomatoes and peppers to develop the best regional variations of those varieties.

The nice thing about heirloom gardening (besides the crazy variety of fruits and vegetables you can get, and their good taste, etc. etc.) is that you can buy seeds once – and then keep collecting them year after year. It's the ultimate in cheapskate gardening. (P.S. You are not a cheapskate. You are fiscally responsible.)

In hybrid varieties, the seeds will not grow true to form. So if you buy a nice hybrid tomato, then plant the seeds next year, you won't get the same fruit, but some variation of the parent plant. But with heirloom seeds, you can save the seeds and get the exact same results year after year after year.

Saving peas and beans and other heirloom vegetables is pretty straightforward. But tomatoes are a different story. You have to separate the seeds from the jelly they're floating in and dry them out.

Clean any dirt off your tomato, then cut your tomato in half across the middle (that is, across the equator of the tomato) and squeeze the tomato seeds, pulp, and juice into a container. A more effective way is to cut off the bottom of the tomato, then squeezing or milking out the germplasm gel containing the seeds off the central column of the fruit.

Make sure the container is labeled with the name of the tomato variety it contains, if you are saving more than one. (If you forgot to do this beforehand, just write the name on a piece of masking tape and slap it on there.) Smaller containers will be fine for a home gardener, like Mason jars or a clean cottage cheese containers – just as long as they have lids.

Now be warned: This next part of the process will stink, so if you have an out of the way place, keep your jars there.\

Fermentation

The tomato seeds will have to go through a fermentation process. This process will remove germination inhibitors. (Seeds can't go germinating willy-nilly, so they have to lock the process. So, to successfully get a seed to germinate, you have to first remove these inhibitors.)

Once you've collected your tomato goop, label (a piece of masking tape is fine) and set the containers in a place where the temperatures stay at 70 degrees or cooler. They'll stay here for one or two days. No more than three days, though, as longer fermentation will cause germination rates to go down.

For the next one or two days, you'll need to stir the tomato goop and submerge the pulpy material, once or twice a day. This will keep mold from building up. The mold doesn't harm the seeds though it will discolor them.

After three days, pour them into a larger container that will allow you to add three times the volume of water (or more). Pour off the pulpy water but not the seeds at the bottom, as the viable tomato seeds will sink to the bottom of the jar. Keep adding water and pouring off the pulp until the seeds are clean.

Then pour the seeds onto an old window screen (for large operations) or some kind of sieve (for home gardeners). Using a spray bottle of water, spray off any goop or debris. Use little squirts of water from the spray bottle to spread the seeds out, as the wet seeds will stick to your hand. Let the seeds dry there for five or six days. Have a little fan going to circulate the air. If you have a large number of seeds, then once a day, stir and rub the seeds together to keep them from sticking in clumps. You can rub the seeds between your hands once they dry a little bit – this helps keep from sticking together.

Another method is just to dry the seeds on a paper plate for a week or two, until they feel dry and papery. Write the name of the variety on each plate so you don't get them mixed up.

Once the tomato seeds are dry, you can store in a labeled zip lock bag, seed envelopes, or a small container in a cool, dark place. You can also store seeds in the fridge. Do not freeze them, however, as that will kill them. Seeds kept this way will store for 4 to 6 years.

If you plan to use your tomato seeds within the next year or two, then you can simply squeeze out the tomato gel, separate out the seeds with a table knife, then dry them on paper plates.

Or, dry the tomato seeds for several weeks on paper towels. Then you can fold up the towel and stick it in a labeled envelope until next spring. When it's time to plant, tear off bits of paper towel with the required number of seeds on it and tuck it into the ground. No fuss, no feathers.

WORK OF THE SEASON

FREE GARDENING BOOK PREVIEWS

I have a few other gardening books I've written (so far) – so here are a couple of sample chapters from them.

This first preview is from my book about vegetable gardening, called _Don't Throw in the Trowel: Vegetable Gardening Month by Month_.

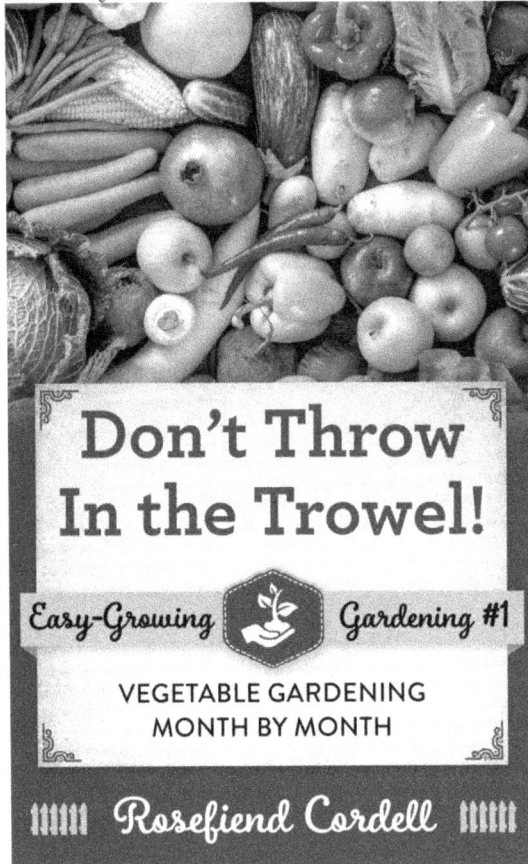

(it looks a lot prettier in color, I swear)

JANUARY

Save Time and Trouble With Garden Journals

When I worked as a municipal horticulturist, I took care of twelve high-maintenance gardens, and a number of smaller ones, over I-don't-know-how-many square miles of city, plus several hundred small trees, an insane number of shrubs, a greenhouse, and whatever else the bosses threw at me. I had to find a way to stay organized besides waking up at 3 a.m. to make extensive lists. My solution: keep a garden journal.

Vegetable gardeners with an organized journal can take control of production and yields. Whether you have a large garden or a small organic farm, it certainly helps to keep track of everything in order to beat the pests, make the most of your harvest, and keep up with spraying and fertilizing.

Keeping a garden journal reduces stress because your overtaxed brain won't have to carry around all those lists. It saves time by keeping you focused. Writing sharpens the mind, helps it to retain more information, and opens your eyes to the world around you.

My journal is a small five-section notebook, college ruled, and I leave it open to the page I'm working on at the time. The only drawback with a spiral notebook is that after a season or two I have to thumb through a lot of pages to find an earlier comment. A small three-ring binder with five separators would do the trick, too. If you wish, you can take out pages at the end of each season and file them in a master notebook.

I keep two notebooks – one for ornamentals and one for vegetables. However, you might prefer to pile everything into one notebook. Do what feels comfortable to you.

These are the five sections I divide my notebooks into – though you might use different classifications, or put them in different orders. Don't sweat it; this ain't brain surgery. Feel free to experiment. You'll eventually settle into the form that suits you best.

First section: To-do lists.

This is pretty self-explanatory: you write a list, you cross off almost everything on it, you make a new list.

When I worked as horticulturist, I did these lists every month. I'd visit all the gardens I took care of. After looking at anything left unfinished on the previous month's list, and looking at the garden to see what else needed to be done, I made a new, comprehensive list.

Use one page of the to-do section for reminders of things you need to do next season. If it's summer, and you think of some chores you'll need to do this fall, make a FALL page and write them down. Doing this has saved me lots of headaches.

Second section: Reference lists.

These are lists that you'll refer back to on occasion.

For example, I'd keep a list of all the yews in the parks system that needed trimmed, a list of all gardens that needed weekly waterings, a list of all places that needed sprayed for bagworms, a list of all the roses that needed to be babied, etc.

I would also keep my running lists in this section, too – lists I keep adding to.

For instance, I kept a list of when different vegetables were ready for harvest – even vegetables I didn't grow, as my friends and relatives reported to me. Then when I made a plan for my veggie garden, I would look at the list to get an idea of when these plants finished up, and then I could figure out when I could take them out and put in a new crop. I also had a list of "seed-to-harvest" times, so I could give each crop enough time to make the harvest date before frost.

You can also keep a wish list – plants and vegetables you'd like to have in your garden.

Third section: Tracking progress.

This is a weekly (or, "whenever it occurs to me to write about it") section as well.

If you plant seeds in a greenhouse, keep track of what seeds you order, when you plant them, when they germinate, how many plants you transplant (and how many survive to maturity), and so forth.

When you finish up in the greenhouse, use these pages to look back and record your thoughts – "I will never again try to start vinca from seeds! Never!! Never!!!" Then you don't annoy yourself by forgetting and buying vinca seeds next year.

You can do the same thing when you move on to the vegetable garden – what dates you tilled the ground, planted the seeds, when they germinated, and so forth. Make notes on yields and how everything tasted. "The yellow crooknecks were definitely not what I'd hoped for. Try yellow zucchini next year."

Be sure to write a vegetable garden overview at season's end, too. "Next year, for goodness' sake, get some 8-foot poles for the beans! Also, drive the poles deeper into the ground so they don't fall over during thunderstorms."

During the winter, you can look back on this section and see ways you can improve your yields and harvest ("The dehydrator worked great on the apples!"), and you can see which of your experiments worked.

Fourth section: Details of the natural world.

When keeping a journal, don't limit yourself to what's going on in your garden. Track events in the natural world, too. Write down when the poplars start shedding cotton or when the Queen's Anne Lace blooms.

You've heard old gardening maxims such as "plant corn when oak leaves are the size of a squirrel's ear," or "prune roses when the forsythia blooms." If the spring has been especially cold and everything's behind, you can rely on nature's cues instead of a calendar when planting or preventing disease outbreaks.

Also, by setting down specific events, you can look at the journal later and say, "Oh, I can expect little caterpillars to attack the indigo plant when the Johnson's Blue geranium is blooming." Then next year, when you notice the buds on your geraniums, you can seek out the caterpillar eggs and squish them before they hatch. An ounce of prevention, see?

When I read back over this section of the journal, patterns start to emerge. I noticed that Stargazer lilies bloom just as the major heat begins. This is no mere coincidence: It's happened for the last three years! So now when I see the large buds, I give the air conditioner a quick checkup.

Fifth section: Notes and comments.

This is more like the journal that most people think of as being a journal – here, you just talk about the garden, mull over how things are looking, or grouse about those supposedly blight-resistant tomatoes that decided to be contrary and keel over from blight.

I generally put a date on each entry, then ramble on about any old thing. You can write a description of the garden at sunset, sketch your peppers, or keep track of the habits of bugs you see crawling around in the plants. This ain't art, this is just fun stuff (which, in the end, yields great dividends).

Maybe you've been to a garden talk on the habits of Asian melons and you need a place to put your notes. Put them here!

This is a good place to put garden plans, too. Years later I run into them again, see old mistakes I've made, and remember neat ideas I haven't tried yet.

Get a calendar.

Then, when December comes, get next year's calendar and the gardening journal and sit down at the kitchen table. Using last year's notes, mark on the calendar events to watch out for -- when the tomatoes first ripen, when the summer heat starts to break, and when you expect certain insects to attack. In the upcoming year, you just look at the calendar and say, "Well, the squash bugs will be hatching soon," so you put on your garden gloves and start smashing the little rafts of red eggs on the plants.

A garden journal can be a fount of information, a source of memories, and most of all, a way to keep organized. Who thought a little spiral notebook could do so much?

If you enjoy the Vegetable Gardening sample, grab a copy! It's available as a paperback and as an ebook.

Now a sample chapter from my book on roses:
Rose to the Occasion: An Easy-Growing Guide to Rose Gardening.

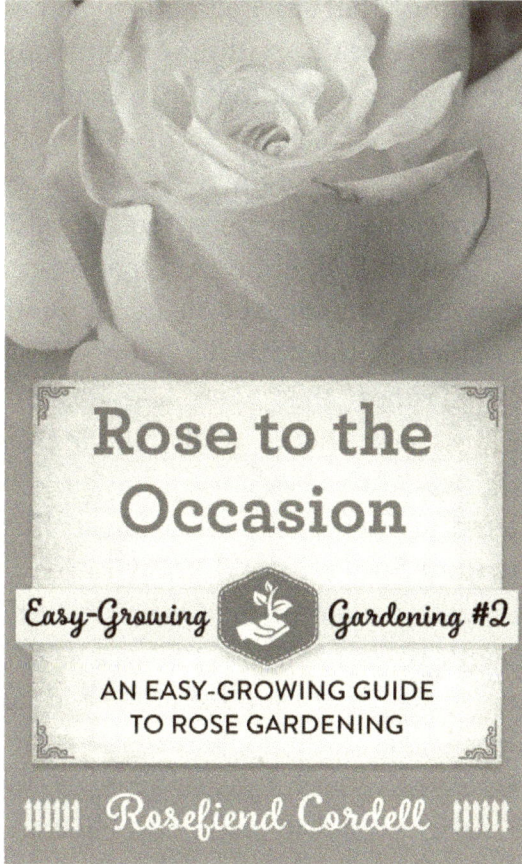

Rose to the Occasion

Easy-Growing Gardening #2

AN EASY-GROWING GUIDE
TO ROSE GARDENING

Rosefiend Cordell

INTRODUCTION

When I started working as city horticulturist, I took care of a bunch of gardens around the city, including the big Krug Park rose garden. It included a bunch of the usual scrawny tea roses, some shrub roses, and a bunch of bare ground.

At the time I was more of a perennials gal, but when I looked at the roses, some of them were really nice. The 'Carefree Delight' roses were covered with rumpled pink blossoms. There was a tall 'Mr. Lincoln' rose and some 'Double Delights' that smelled amazing. A bunch of 'Scarlet Meidilands' were really putting on a blooming show, with tiny scarlet flowers cascading all over them. Not shabby at all.

I started taking care of the roses, but I noticed that a lot of the 'Scarlet Meidilands' were sprouting odd growths. Most of the new growth looked fine, with bronzed, flat leaves that looked attractive. But some of the new growth was markedly different – skinny, stunted leaves with pebbled surfaces, and hyperthorny canes that were downright rubbery. The blossoms on these shoots were crinkled and didn't open worth a darn.

I hollered at Charles Anctil, a Master Rosarian with the American Rose Society. We'd known each other since 1992 when we both worked at the Old Mill Nursery. He'd been working with roses for a good 50 years, and he knows his stuff. At any rate, Charles looked over the roses and told me that those roses, and others, had rose rosette virus, a highly contagious disease, and a death sentence for a rose. Every one of those roses had to come out. He couldn't believe the extent of the damage. He said that he had never seen so many roses infected by rose rosette in one place.

Oh great! Why do I get to be the lucky one?

I dug up many roses that spring. That winter, I got a work crew and dug up 50 more. I had to replace all those roses, so I started researching new varieties.

As city horticulturist with no staff, I was already running like hell everywhere I went, so I wanted roses that wouldn't wilt or croak or wrap themselves in blackspot every time I looked at them cross-eyed. I wanted tough roses, roses that took heat and drought and bug attacks and zombie apocalypses with aplomb and would still come out looking great and covered with scented blossoms. (And the blossoms HAD to be scented – there was no two ways about that.)

I started reading rose catalogs. I talked to Charles some more, which is always fun. Somewhere along the way, I got obsessed. I immersed myself in roses. That's how I learn – I get excited about a subject and start reading everything in sight about it, as if it's a mini-course in school. I read about antique roses, which were making a comeback. Different rose breeders, most notably David Austin, were crossing modern varieties with old varieties and to get roses that combined the best of the new and the old. Other breeders were creating roses that were tough and disease-resistant, such as the 'Knock-Out' landscape rose, which now you see everywhere.

I planted some antique roses, and they looked great. I planted more. The rose garden was starting to look spiffy, even though I still had to take roses out every year due to the rose rosette virus. I even tucked in some annuals and perennials around the garden to doll up the place when the roses conked out in July and August.

Roses are amazing plants. Many old roses have a long and storied history. Some species that were growing during the time of the Pyramids are still blooming today. And these roses are attractive and fragrant. What could be better?

Some people say that you can't grow roses organically. I say you can. I did use a few chemicals when I was a horticulturist, but that was because I had a huge list of things to do in a limited amount of time. I used Round Up for spot-weeding (a tiny squirt for each weed, just enough to wet the leaves), a systemic granular fungicide to keep up with blackspot, and Miracle-Gro as part of the fertilizing regimen for convenience.

If you choose to use chemicals, use them responsibly. Don't spray them and expect the problem to be fixed. They work best when you combine them with other control methods. I'll give you an example that's not rose-related. I had a mandevilla plant in the greenhouse that had a huge mealybug problem. (Mealybugs are a small, white insect that sucks out plant juices. The young bugs look like bits of cotton.) I sprayed the plant with insecticide until the leaves were dripping. The mealybugs were still there. I put a systemic insecticide around the roots of the plant and watered it in. The mealybugs didn't care.

So I just started squishing the mealybugs with my fingers, a gross job because they squirt orange goo. At that point, I didn't care. I searched them out and squashed them where they were cuddled up around buds, in the cracks of the plant, and under the leaves. I even found some on the roots just under the soil. I squished those and added a little extra potting soil. I checked the plant every other day and squished every mealybug I could find. After a while, I stopped finding them altogether. Then I fertilized the plant, and the mandevilla put out leaves like crazy and started blooming. Success!

Chemicals aren't a cure-all by any means. They're convenient, but sometimes you just have to get in and do a little hands-on work with the plant to help it along. It's a good feeling when a plant you've been working with rights itself and perks up again.

Though I'm no longer a horticulturist, I wrote this book because I have worked in horticulture for about half my life, and have a decent understanding about how the natural world works. I might possibly be just a little crazy about roses. I hope my experiences are helpful and that you're able to benefit from them – and that your roses benefit as well.

The end of the sample.
Rose to the Occasion is available in ebook, paperback, and audio!

Sample chapter from *Design of the Times: How to Plan Glorious Landscapes and Gardens*

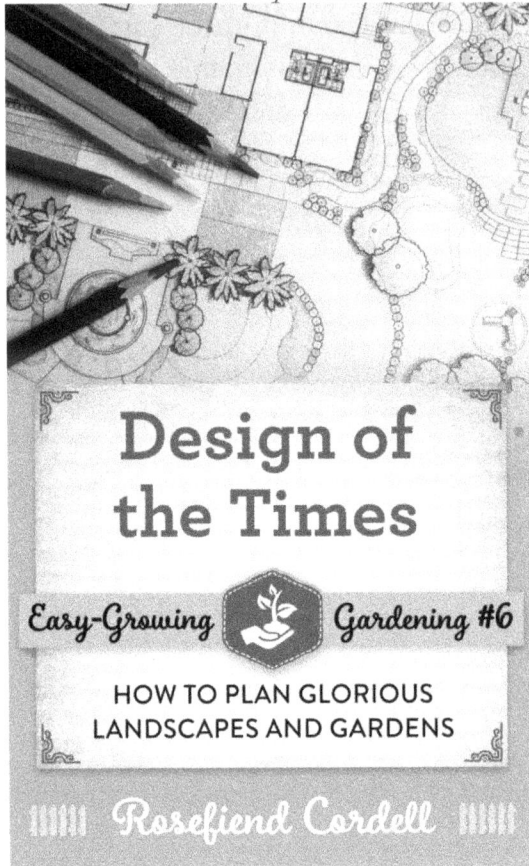

Rules of (Green) Thumb for Garden Design

Once you have all your garden measured out, sit down with your graph paper, let one square equal one square foot (adjust this if you have the graph paper with the tiny squares), and start putting this all down on paper. Have the top of the paper be north, and draw a little arrow pointing that way to look more official.

As you do, you will find that you'll need to keep running out to measure more things in the yard in order to make everything line up correctly. You've measured the house and driveway, for example, but wait, how many feet do you have between the driveway and the east corner of the house? So you measure that. Where exactly does the oak tree sit in relation to the fence and the house? So you measure that. The fence and the house are not lining up correctly. So you remeasure that and try to figure out if you transposed a measurement. The oak tree seems to have inadvertently shrunk, though you'd measured it twice. Maybe it's time to take up drinking. Well, okay, but only in moderation.

Of course, that's the way the old timers did it. (Note: I am not old.) These days, you can fix up a nice landscape plan on your phone using an app, or get a more elaborate program for your laptop that will do more than just move a tree symbol around until it looks like it's placed right.

Get the whole family involved with planning your garden!

Then it's time for the big step: drawing a plan. Measure your garden. To keep your plan simple, let one-half inch equal one foot. Draw the outline of the garden on your paper.

Protip: Once you have this step finished to your satisfaction, take this paper to the copier and make several copies, and use these as the rough drafts of your garden design.

Now play with that outline. Consider the height and width of these plants. Keep short plants in front and tall plants in back, and use those pictures you've clipped (whether out of a magazine or found on the internet) to make sure the colors match. Do you want soft colors, such as purple catmint, pink petunias, and silver Artemisia? Or do you want a fiesta of red salvia and "Yellow Boy" marigolds?

Also, consider when your perennials bloom. You may love purple asters and pink sea thrift, but that color pairing won't be happening, because the asters bloom in fall and the sea thrift blooms in spring.

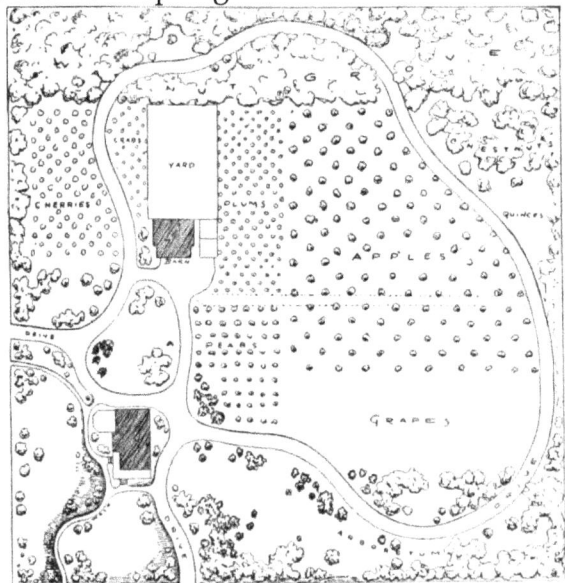

It's a good idea to put the tall plants in back and short plants in front. Green side up. Match the plants to the amount of sun that's available. Set your shade plants near the trees, while the full sun plants will need to be right out in the sun.

As you draw your plan, generally a good rule of thumb is to arrange them by height – tallest plants in back, shortest ones in the back. Or, as with an island bed, tallest plants in the middle, going to the shortest on the edges. But you can also blend several different varieties of plants that are the same size, the same way as you would blend several different flowers in a flower arrangement, for a good blend of colors and shapes. And you don't have to be exact on regimenting sizes. A garden isn't a lineup of soldiers on dress parade, after all.

You can arrange the plants in any way. You can arrange them in a parterre, a formal setting with neat rows, tidy edged shrubs. Or you can have a wild, natural garden with plants arranged as if they were growing wild. Chances are you will be someplace between these two extremes in your own garden.

Also, to make more of an impact, plant your perennials in drifts of 3, 5, or 7. These groups provide more of an impact than just planting one of every plant (unless you have a specimen plant that's as big as an elephant).

Protip: It's a good idea to have a little out-of-the-way place in your garden where you keep extra plants – those you've picked up when on sale but can't find a place for, plants you've picked up out of curiosity, plants you've gotten from friends and neighbors that don't quite fit into your gardening plan, or things you need to find a proper place for but haven't gotten to yet.

This little garden can get helpful, though. If you have a plant in your regular garden that suddenly croaks, you can grab a full-grown specimen from your little side garden and pop it into your regular garden, if you're so inclined, thereby filling the gap.

You can also keep your cutting garden here, so you can just pop out the back door and cut a few flowers for bouquets inside the house. Then you won't have to swipe flowers from your front gardens and leave holes in it.

Design of the Times is available in ebook, paperback, and as an audiobook.

Me in 1995, when I embarked upon the grand adventure
of being a published author.
I was kind of a writing hotshot back then.
If you want to be perfectly honest, I still am.

ABOUT THE AUTHOR

I've worked in most all aspects of horticulture – garden centers, wholesale greenhouses, as a landscape designer, and finally as city horticulturist, where I took care of 20+ gardens around the city. I live in northwest Missouri with my husband and kids, the best little family that ever walked the earth. In 2012, when I was hugely pregnant, I graduated from Hamline University with a master's of writing for children; three weeks later, I had a son. It was quite a time.

My first book, **Courageous Women of the Civil War: Soldiers, Spies, Medics, and More** was published by Chicago Review Press in August 2016. This is a series of profiles of women who fought or cared for the wounded during the Civil War.

I've been sending novels out to publishers and agents since 1995, and have racked up I don't know how many hundreds of rejections. I kept getting very close – but not close enough. Agents kept saying, "You're a very good writer, you have an excellent grasp of craft, but I just don't feel that 'spark'...." Even after *Courageous Women* was published, they still weren't interested in my books.

In September 2016, I rage-quit traditional publishing and started self-publishing, because I wanted to get my books out to people who *would* feel that 'spark.' In my first year, I published 15 books. This year I plan to repeat that. (When you've been writing novels for over 20 years, you're going to have a bit of a backlog.) I am working my way completely through it and having a complete blast. I love doing cover work and designing the book interiors. I work full-time as a proofreader, so I handle that in my books as well.

And now I'm finding fans of my books who do feel that 'spark.' They're peaches, every one of them.

I'm finally doing what I was put on this earth to do.

There's no better feeling than that.

If you like this book, please leave a review on my BookBub or Goodreads page. Reviews help me get more readers.

Thanks so much for reading!
melindacordell.com

www.ingramcontent.com/pod-product-compliance
Lightning Source LLC
Chambersburg PA
CBHW032055040426
42335CB00037B/814